UNIVERSITY OF NORTHERN IOWA

3 5035 01 442043 9

D1457158

THE SPACE BOOK

DATE DUE

YOUTH COLLECTION
BROWSING
TO BE CIRCULATED AFTER
DEC 0 4 2008
APR 2 0 2011
DEC 0 7 2011

Withdrawn

THE SPACE BOOK

Activities for Experiencing the Universe and the Night Sky

MARC McCUTCHEON

John Wiley & Sons, Inc.

LIBRARY
UNIVERSITY OF NORTHERN IOWA
CEDAR FALLS, IOWA

Y
520
M
c. 2

This book is printed on acid-free paper. ⊗

Copyright © 2003 by Marc McCutcheon. All rights reserved

Illustrations copyright © 2003 by Tina Cash-Walsh

Photo credits: page 10: D. Roddy/Lunar and Planetary Institute; pages 14, 37, 38, 41, 45, 50, 53, 55, 57, 86: Courtesy of NASA; pages 20 top, 93: NOAO/AURA/NSF; page 20 bottom: Courtesy of Big Bear Solar Observatory; page 27: Courtesy of SOHO/Extreme Ultraviolet Imaging Telescope (EIT) consortium. SOHO is a project of international cooperation between ESA and NASA; page 32: Courtesy of U.S. Geological Survey; page 43 left: Courtesy of NASA and the Hubble Heritage Team (STScI/AURA); pages 43 right, 47, 54: Courtesy of NASA/JPL; page 51: Courtesy of NASA/JPL/University of Arizona; page 58: Courtesy of Alan Stern (Southwest Research Institute), Marc Buie (Lowell Observatory), NASA, and ESA; page 80: Courtesy of National Astronomy and Ionosphere Center, Cornell U., NSF; page 95 bottom: Courtesy of Dave Palmer.

Published by John Wiley & Sons, Inc., Hoboken, New Jersey
Published simultaneously in Canada

Design and production by Navta Associates, Inc.

No part of this publication may be reproduced, stored in a retrieval system, or transmitted in any form or by any means, electronic, mechanical, photocopying, recording, scanning, or otherwise, except as permitted under Section 107 or 108 of the 1976 United States Copyright Act, without either the prior written permission of the Publisher, or authorization through payment of the appropriate per-copy fee to the Copyright Clearance Center, 222 Rosewood Drive, Danvers, MA 01923, (978) 750-8400, fax (978) 750-4744, or on the web at www.copyright.com. Requests to the Publisher for permission should be addressed to the Permissions Department, John Wiley & Sons, Inc., 111 River Street, Hoboken, NJ 07030, (201) 748-6011, fax (201) 748-6008, email: permcoordinator@wiley.com.

The publisher and the author have made every reasonable effort to insure that the experiments and activities in the book are safe when conducted as instructed but assume no responsibility for any damage caused or sustained while performing the experiments or activities in this book. Parents, guardians, and/or teachers should supervise young readers who undertake the experiments and activities in this book.

For general information about our other products and services, please contact our Customer Care Department within the United States at (800) 762-2974, outside the United States at (317) 572-3993 or fax (317) 572-4002.

Wiley also publishes its books in a variety of electronic formats. Some content that appears in print may not be available in electronic books.

Library of Congress Cataloging-in-Publication Data

McCutcheon, Marc
    The space book : activities for experiencing the universe and night sky / Marc McCutcheon.
       p. cm.
    Includes bibliographical references and index.
    ISBN 0-471-16142-X (pbk. : acid-free paper)
      1. Astronomy—Study and teaching (Elementary)   2. Astronomy—Study and teaching—Activity programs.   I. Title.

QB61 .M38 2002
372.3'5—dc21   2002032431

Printed in the United States of America

10 9 8 7 6 5 4 3 2 1

Contents

Introduction 1

PART I EXPLORING OUR SOLAR SYSTEM 3

1 The Moon 5

2 The Sun 17

3 Planets, Asteroids, Comets, and Meteors 31

PART II NEXT STOP: OUTER SPACE 69

4 Stars 71

5 Galaxies, Quasars, and Nebulae 85

6 Extrasolar Planets and the Search 99
for Extraterrestrial Life

Glossary 109

Index 115

THE SPACE BOOK

Our universe is a sorry little affair unless it has in it something for every age to investigate. . . . Nature does not reveal her mysteries once and for all.

Seneca, *Natural Questions*, Book 7 (first century)

Introduction

Gaze up into the night sky and what do you see? Stars, of course. But what are stars? If you lived in ancient times, you may have believed they were drops of milk, red-hot stones, or heavenly torches in the sky.

Today we know they're gigantic balls of gas, just like our Sun. In fact, stars are just that—suns. They look small to us only because they are so very far away.

Not all stars are alike. Shimmering yellow. Blazing blue. Scintillating red. They may be as small as a city or, in some cases, hundreds of times as large as our own Sun.

Some "dead" stars are actually invisible. On these lifeless cinders, gravity is so powerful that even light is unable to escape.

To the casual observer, the night sky is remarkably deceptive. Sometimes objects that look like stars are not stars at all, but planets. The planets Mars, Venus, Jupiter, and Saturn often look like the brightest "stars" in the sky. But planets are actually much smaller than most stars, and they don't generate their own light like stars do. Instead planets shine because the light from our Sun is reflected off their surfaces, just like our Moon.

Still other starlike objects are neither stars nor planets, but galaxies. Galaxies are gatherings of millions and even billions of suns. To the naked eye or under low resolution through a telescope, they may appear only as dim, fuzzy lights. Peer through a stronger telescope, however, and you may see something truly spectacular.

And look up there. What's that light moving across the sky? A comet? A meteor? A satellite? An alien spaceship?

In space there is just so much to see and explore, so much to marvel over and wonder about.

The cosmos. The universe. The great beyond. It doesn't matter what we call it. Words will never adequately describe it. For it is a tantalizing and largely unexplored mystery, a treasure box full of surprises and weirdness just waiting for us to open and study it.

It's only possible to understand space a little bit at a time. Thus we'll begin our exploration in our own backyard: the planets and satellites of our solar system. From there we'll venture out into the vast regions of our universe. By the end of our journey, we still won't know all there is to know about space. That's because so much of it is yet to be discovered and explored.

Scientists say it's a place that may go on forever. Forever.

Can you imagine a place that never ends? A place in which you can travel at the speed of a flashlight beam for a billion years and still not arrive anywhere near its edge?

If only one place deserves to be described as awesome, this is it.

Space.

Let's go.

Part I

EXPLORING OUR SOLAR SYSTEM

Pack a big lunch. Put on your spacesuit and helmet. Say goodbye to your family. We're about to take a tour of the universe—starting with our solar system—and we may not be back for a while. The **solar system** is made up of the Sun and all the planets, moons, asteroids, comets, and debris that orbit around it.

Step into our flight deck and strap in. Comfy? You'd better be. You're going to be in this chair for a loooooooooonnnnnnng time.

The spaceship we'll be riding in today is no ordinary rocket. It's capable of traveling faster than the speed of light. The speed of light is 186,000 miles (300,000 km) per second. No spaceship humans have ever designed can go anywhere near this fast. Nor, say scientists, is such a feat even possible. Yet space is so incredibly vast that anything slower would take an eternity to get us to where we need to go. (Today's fastest spaceships would take 40,000 years to reach the nearest star.) Our ship, then, is powered by a fuel called imagination.

The Moon

L et's begin our exploration with our closest neighbor—the one and only celestial neighbor humans have stepped foot upon. A place science fiction writer Arthur C. Clarke called "the first milestone on the way to the stars."

The Moon.
10, 9, 8, 7, 6, 5, 4, 3, 2, 1 . . .
We're off!

FIGURE IT OUT

Good astronauts figure out their flight plan far in advance. If the speed of light is 186,000 miles (300,000 km) per second, how far will our spaceship travel in a minute? An hour? Use a pencil and paper, a calculator (if it will display numbers high enough), or a computer to figure it out.

As we blast off from Earth, g forces will drive you back into your chair more powerfully than a dentist threatening with his drill. One thing you'll discover quickly: getting into space is uncomfortable. Just imagine the weight of a walrus bearing down on your chest.

"G force" is a fancy term for gravity. Gravity, of course, is the irresistible "pull" produced by any large mass, such as the Earth. It's the force that keeps your feet planted on the ground. It also makes things fall "down" instead of "up."

Earth isn't the only celestial body that has gravity. The Moon produces its own gravity, as do the Sun and planets. Even buildings have masses large enough to generate gravity effects. A ball dropped from the top of a skyscraper, for example, will actually fall *toward* the building.

The biggest challenge all spaceship designers face is producing a force strong enough to defeat gravity. Historically, they've done it just one way—by constructing a vessel that is, in reality, a bomb that explodes a little at a time.

To escape Earth's iron grip, our spaceship must achieve a speed of 25,000 miles (40,000 km) per hour. But once we've gotten off Earth, our trip to the Moon will be a short one. If you flash a flashlight beam at the Moon from Earth, it will reach the Moon's surface in less than one and a half seconds. Because our imaginary spaceship can travel at the same speed, the speed of light, we too will reach the Moon in one and a half seconds. In fact, we're already there.

The Moon's Phases

The near side of the Moon may be wholly or partially lit by the Sun. How much of the Moon we see depends on where it is in its orbit around Earth. An **orbit** is the elliptical (oval) path one body follows as it revolves around another body.

Over a roughly 14-day cycle the Moon reveals more and more of its surface. When its orbit takes it *between* the Sun and Earth, the Moon becomes invisible. It's still there, of course, but the side facing us is dark. Rule of thumb: If it's not lit by the Sun, we cannot see it. Oddly enough, this invisible phase is called the **new Moon.**

The Moon's Phases

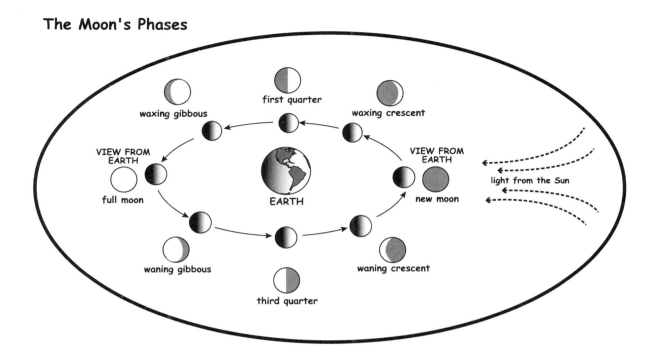

As the Moon continues in its orbit, its sunlit side gradually begins to appear to us again. The first sliver we notice is called a crescent Moon. The Moon is now entering its waxing (increasing or brightening) phase.

As the Moon moves away from the Sun and proceeds in its orbit around Earth, the waxing increases. This happens because the angle of sunlight reaching the Moon changes. The crescent grows to a quarter Moon, a half Moon, a three-quarter Moon, and, finally, a full Moon.

The Moon is full only when Earth is between the Sun and the Moon. After full Moon, the phases are repeated in reverse. Then the Moon is waning (decreasing or growing dimmer).

SEE WHY THE MOON WAXES AND WANES

You can demonstrate the Moon's phases and why we can't see the new Moon.

WHAT YOU NEED   flashlight

softball or baseball

golf ball

1 In a dark corner of your home, take the flashlight, turn it on, and place it on a stand or table. The flashlight is the Sun. Hold the softball in front of the light. The softball is Earth.

2 Now take the golf ball (its dimples make nice craters) and move it into different positions around the softball. The golf ball is the Moon.

3 Notice how much or how little of the flashlight's (the Sun's) light falls on the golf ball, depending on where you place it in relation to the softball (Earth). Experiment until you can create the phases of the Moon (illuminating one-quarter, one-half, then full) on your ball.

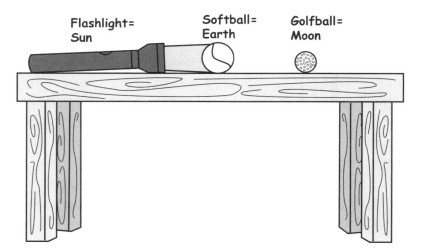

Flashlight= Sun   Softball= Earth   Golfball= Moon

4 Finally, hold the golf ball between the flashlight (Sun) and the softball (Earth). Notice the unlit or dark side facing Earth? This dark side is the new Moon. We can't see a new Moon because the side facing us is completely dark.

What's a lunar eclipse?

An **eclipse** is the obscuring of one celestial object by another. A full lunar eclipse occurs when Earth is positioned between the Sun and the Moon and the three celestial bodies line up exactly. When this happens, Earth's shadow falls on the Moon, making it nearly invisible to us.

But not always. Often during an eclipse a small portion of sunlight filters through Earth's atmosphere and illuminates the Moon

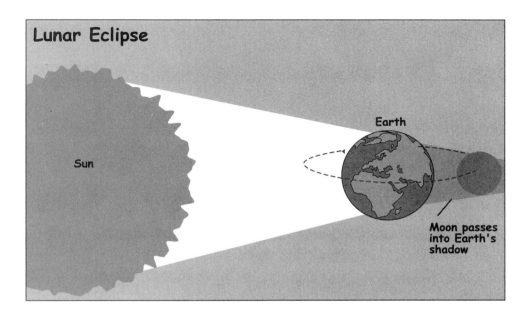

Lunar Eclipse

Sun

Earth

Moon passes
into Earth's
shadow

with a dull red or orange color. As the Moon moves out of Earth's shadow, its reflected light and color gradually return to normal.

During a partial lunar eclipse, only part of the Moon may be obscured by Earth's shadow.

Why don't we see a lunar eclipse every time the Moon is in its full phase?

Because the Moon's path is not always deep enough behind Earth to hide it completely from the Sun. This lack of precise alignment is the same reason we don't see a solar eclipse (when the Moon is between the Sun and Earth) every time the Moon is in its new phase.

The Moon Close Up

Whether crescent or full, one thing about this charcoal-gray sphere strikes the eye immediately: it looks as if it has survived a war.

For eons, space rocks called meteoroids and asteroids (for more on those see chapter 3) have missiled in from all over the solar system. They've pocked the Moon's landscape with upward of half a million **craters.** These impact holes range in size from swimming pools to baseball stadiums to canyons more than 150 miles (240 km) across. Some are as deep as mountains are tall.

The Moon's Features

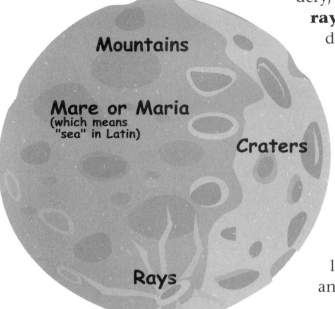

Mountains

Mare or Maria
(which means
"sea" in Latin)

Craters

Rays

Radiating out from these great chasms are powdery, light-colored lines of ejected matter, called **rays.** Clearly seen from Earth, they show how devastating an asteroid's impact power can be.

You may be tempted to call the Moon "magnificent desolation," as astronauts before you have. In fact, Neil Armstrong (b. 1930), the first astronaut ever to step foot on its surface, said, "It has a stark beauty of its own. It's much like the high desert of the United States. It's different, but it's very pretty here."

Yet there is no escaping the truth. The Moon is a cold and miserable place, with no liquid surface water, no air to breathe, no wind, and no life-forms of any kind.

Why isn't Earth covered with craters like the Moon?

Actually, Earth has been struck many times by large asteroids and meteorites. But most of the craters that resulted are now under water or filled in with rock. About 150 craters can today be found in many areas of Earth. The best known in the United States is probably the 4,100-foot (1,230-m)–wide, 571-foot (1,713 m)–deep Meteor Crater in the Arizona desert. It was created by the impact

of a 70,000-ton (63,000-t) meteorite between 30,000 and 50,000 years ago.

Unlike the craters on the Moon, the craters on Earth are often hidden by thick jungles or large bodies of water. Those that aren't covered over usually end up being eroded away by the forces of wind, weather, and volcanic activity.

The Moon has no weather, and its volcanoes are all now dormant, so its craters can remain intact for billions of years.

The Moon's Mountains and "Seas"

As we move closer in our orbit, the Moon's mountains, valleys, and ridges loom into view. We pass over sweeping dark plains called **maria.** People once thought maria were vast oceans. In fact, *mare* is from the Latin for "sea." That's why several large regions on the Moon, including Oceanus Procellarum ("Ocean of Storms") and Mare Tranquillitatis ("Sea of Tranquility"), are called "seas," even though they contain no water.

In reality, these great expanses—one of them twice as large as the state of Texas—are giant impact craters filled in by ancient lava flows.

MAKE YOUR OWN MOONSCAPE

You can make your own moonscape.

WHAT YOU NEED   large baking pan

newspaper

mud or plaster of paris (plaster of paris will quickly harden into a permanent model)

plastic spoon

1 Place the baking pan over a few sheets of newspaper to avoid a mess. Fill the pan with mud. If you are using plaster of paris, follow package directions carefully.

2 Before the mud or plaster in the pan hardens, use a plastic spoon to fling spoonfuls of more mud or plaster onto the surface of the mud or plaster in the pan—the surface of the model Moon. The harder you flick with your spoon, the deeper the craters will be. Experiment with different spoonful sizes and taking shots from different angles to represent variously sized asteroids coming from different points of space.

The Moon's Far Side and Gravity

As we rocket around the Moon, we finally get a chance to eyeball its ominous far side. Even though the Moon revolves, this mysterious far side is never visible to Earthlings. That's because the time it takes the Moon to complete one rotation is, coincidentally, the same time it takes the Moon to orbit Earth.

Not that there is much to see here on the far side anyway. A Soviet space probe called *Luna 3* provided the first glimpse of the

Moon's far side in 1959. Contrary to what some tabloid newspapers may report, there are no alien bases here. Just a lot more craters.

Because the Moon is about a quarter the size of Earth, its gravity is weaker. In general, the larger a planet's or moon's mass, the stronger its gravity.

Because the Moon's gravity is less than Earth's, everything weighs less on the Moon than it does on Earth. For example, if you weigh 90 pounds (40.5 kg) on Earth, you'd weigh about 15 pounds (6.75 kg) on the Moon. No question about it, most kids could easily leap high enough to slam-dunk a basketball here.

Because the Moon's pull is so much weaker, it will be much easier for our spaceship to escape from it than from the pull of Earth.

FAST FACTS about the MOON

Average Distance from Earth: about 238,900 miles (384,390 km).

Diameter: 2,160 miles (3,476 km), slightly more than a quarter of Earth's size. If it could be placed over the United States, the Moon would span from Cleveland, Ohio, to San Francisco, California.

Surface: The lunar surface is littered with rocks and boulders. Its "soil" is actually composed of hardened lava, crushed rock fragments, and glass.

Surface Temperature: about –280° (–173°C) to 250° (121°C), depending on how much of the Sun's rays hit the surface.

Light: The Moon does not make its own light. Instead it shines by reflecting light from the Sun.

Tides: The Moon is the main factor in the creation of tides on Earth. (The Sun plays a role in the tides as well, but its influence is not as great because it is so far away.) Strange as it may sound, the Moon actually pulls water on Earth toward it. Thus water at high tide is closest to the Moon, while water at low tide is farthest away. Two cycles of high and low tides occur each day as the Moon travels eastward around Earth.

Smallest Craters Visible from Earth: The smallest craters we can see with a telescope from Earth are about ½ mile (800 m) in diameter.

Best Time to View through Binoculars: The Moon is best viewed during any of its partial phases, rather than during its full phase. Contrasts are much deeper and details more sharply defined when the Moon is partly darkened.

Where on earth did the Moon come from?

Where on Earth, indeed. The most widely accepted theory is that the Moon originated from vaporized matter that was blown off after Earth collided with a Mars-sized body billions of years ago. This matter gradually came together to form the Moon we know today.

Scientists have come up with other ideas. Can you think of any other possibilities?

What's a blue Moon?

The term **blue Moon** has several meanings. One is the appearance of a second full Moon in one month. That happens once in about every two and a half years.

Another kind of blue Moon occurs when massive amounts of smoke—such as from a forest fire or volcanic eruption—rise high into Earth's atmosphere. The smoke acts as a kind of color filter, making the Moon take on a bluish hue.

Both occurrences happen only once in a while. This is why, when someone says something only happens "once in a blue moon," they mean it's a rare thing.

FIGURE IT OUT

From a spaceship, it's easy to see that Earth is not flat but round. In ancient times, it was impossible to see Earth from such a vantage point. On the ground, Earth looks and feels flat. How, then, did early scientists figure out that Earth was really a globe?

Long before Christopher Columbus (1451–1506) came along, several scientists had figured it out. Can you think of the things the ancient scientists looked at to prove Earth's "roundness"? If you can figure it out, you're probably a lot sharper than the average adult. Try studying the Moon for a start. Then check page 16 for some tantalizing clues.

SEE HOW THE MOON PULLS AT OUR OCEANS

You can use magnets to help illustrate how the Moon's gravity pulls at Earth's oceans and creates the tides.

WHAT YOU NEED   as many metal pins, needles, and small nails as you can find

dinner plate

large magnet

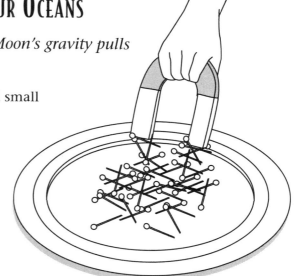

Place the pins, needles, and nails in the center of the plate, then pass the magnet (the Moon) over the top of this "pin" ocean and watch what happens. *Voilà!* A tide!

Look for Earthshine

Carefully examine the next slender crescent Moon you see. If your neighborhood is sufficiently dark, you should be able to notice that the unlit or "dark" portion of the Moon is not completely dark. Rather, it's slightly illuminated by a dull light. Believe it or not, that light is the reflected light of Earth. It's called earthshine.

Earthshine is difficult to see as the Moon's crescent grows. And its intensity can vary from month to month. Generally, earthshine is brightest when the part of Earth facing the Sun is cloudiest. Clouds are highly reflective, and when sunlight bounces off them, more of the light reaches the Moon to illuminate it.

If your sky is polluted by city lights, try to find earthshine through a pair of binoculars.

One last interesting tidbit before we leave for our next destination. Before life began on Earth, the Moon was as close as 14,000 miles (22,530 km) away and filled a whopping one-quarter of the night sky. That must have been a truly breathtaking sight. Yet today the Moon appears far tinier and fills only a fraction of the sky it once did. Why? The Moon is slowly escaping from its orbit around Earth. In fact, it moves away from us about 1 inch (2.54 cm) every year.

Using the inch-per-year estimate, how many feet, meters, miles, or kilometers closer would the Moon have been a billion years ago? If your calculator won't go to a billion, you'll have to figure it out on paper.

Next stop: the Sun. Air conditioner set to *full blast!*

Predicting When the Moon Will Rise

You don't have to be psychic to predict when the Moon will rise. Few people realize that the Moon makes its appearance roughly 50 minutes later each night. So if it appears over the horizon at 6:00 P.M. tonight, you won't see it in the same place again until 6:50 P.M. tomorrow.

From our vantage point on Earth, the Moon appears to rise in the east and set in the west, but when measured against the stars, it actually travels in the opposite direction. You can blame Earth's rotation for this very confusing illusion.

Answer to question on page 14.

Clues Ancient Scientists Used to Determine That Earth Is Round

1. The Sun is round. So is the Moon.
2. The shadow of Earth on the Moon during an eclipse is curved.
3. A ship sailing out into the ocean gradually appears to "sink" into the water and vanish in the distance. It isn't sinking, of course. It is simply sailing over the curvature of the horizon. (You can see this same effect when you're on a ship and approach an island with a mountain on it. At first, you can see only the peak. Then more and more of the mountain appears as you get closer, until finally the base appears.)
4. The Sun sets later in western cities than in eastern ones. It also rises earlier in the east. If Earth was flat, the Sun would be seen to set and rise at the same time everywhere.
5. Constellations seen deep in the southern hemisphere cannot be seen in the northern hemisphere and vice versa.

The Sun

Traveling at the speed of light, our spaceship arrives at a roiling globe of gas—the Sun—8.3 minutes after we leave the Moon.

A sunbeam must travel 93 million miles (150 million km) at light speed to reach Earth. Luckily, that distance allows the Sun's heat to cool just enough to make life possible. Can you imagine the heat if Earth were located any closer to the Sun than it is? Or the cold if it were farther away?

The Sun is composed largely of **hydrogen,** with a smaller amount of helium and other elements. Hydrogen is the lightest and most abundant element in the universe. On Earth, hydrogen is found in water. It's also used to make rocket fuels and ammonia. In the past, people used hydrogen to fill dirigibles (blimps) because it is so light. But because it is also very explosive, it was replaced by helium.

In reality, we could not get very close to the Sun and expect to survive. The Sun's heat would fry anything that got near it. But assuming we could get close, one thing would be obvious: the Sun is *huge*.

Saying that the Sun's diameter is 865,000 miles (1,392,000 km) might not mean much. But consider this eye-popping fact: scientists estimate that from 700,000 to 1,000,000 Earths could fit inside of the Sun. In fact the Sun contains 99.86 percent of all of the mass in the solar system.

To us puny humans, this is indeed unimaginably huge.

Because it is so very vast, many people fail to realize that the Sun is actually a **star** (a giant ball of gas that generates energy from nuclear fusion reactions). It only looks larger and brighter to us because it is so much closer than all the other stars. Many stars in the universe are just as big or even bigger. A star called Betelgeuse (pronounced beetle juice) could hold scores of our Suns inside of it. Another star called Epsilon Aurigae (pronounced EP- suh-lahn aw-REYE-guh) could easily contain thousands of our Suns!

SHOW WHY THE SUN APPEARS AS A GLOBE BUT THE STARS LOOK LIKE PINPOINTS OF LIGHT

If they were close enough, stars would look like fiery globes, like our Sun.

WHAT YOU NEED   small flashlight
helper

Have a helper shine the flashlight toward your face at a short distance. From this short distance, it's easy to see the "roundness" of the flashlight's lens. Move it far enough away, however, and the roundness disappears. At long distances only the flashlight's dim pinpoint of light can be seen, exactly like a distant star.

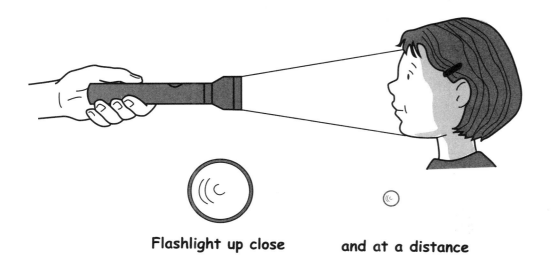

Flashlight up close   **and at a distance**

Like Betelgeuse and Epsilon Aurigae, our Sun also has a name—**Sol.**

Although we know Sol is there and what it is made of, and that it throws off lots of heat and light, no human has ever actually seen the surface of the Sun.

It's true. The Sun is hidden by a thick, hot atmosphere composed of three layers: the **photosphere,** the **chromosphere,** and the outermost part, the **corona.** The corona extends 10 million miles (16 million km) from the Sun itself.

When we look at the Sun, we are actually seeing these layers of gases. Below these gases, the Sun's interior must also be made of gases, because no solid could last at such very high temperatures.

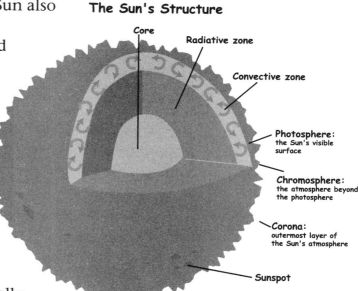

The Sun's Structure

Core

Radiative zone

Convective zone

Photosphere:
the Sun's visible
surface

Chromosphere:
the atmosphere beyond
the photosphere

Corona:
outermost layer of
the Sun's atmosphere

Sunspot

Warning! *Never look directly at the Sun either with the naked eye or with binoculars or a telescope. To do so could cause permanent blindness! Although dark Sun filters are available for use in telescopes, they sometimes shatter.* *See the sunspot activity on page 21 to learn how to view the Sun safely.*

Sunspots and Solar Flares

Because our imaginary ship is equipped with protective dark lenses, it is safe for us to peer out. Look closely at the Sun's surface and immediately you'll notice something strange: spots.

These dark spots are called **sunspots.** Sunspots can be as small as the Moon or many times larger than Earth. Formed by magnetic disturbances in the photosphere, they're darker than surrounding areas because they're cooler. Using ultrasound technology, scientists have discovered huge hurricanes of electrified gas swirling underneath these spots.

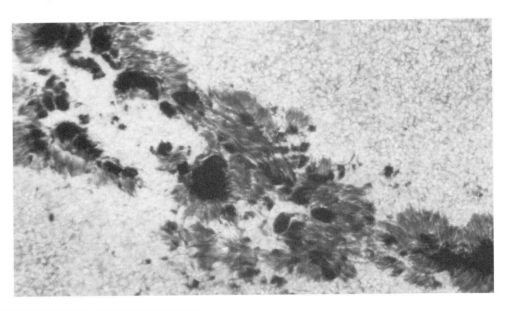

Because the Sun rotates, sunspots appear to move from one side of the surface to the other. Eventually they fade away, only to reappear somewhere else.

Sunspots can sometimes erupt in **solar flares.** Flares look like streams of fire erupting from the Sun. They discharge massive amounts of charged plasma, cosmic rays, X rays, and gamma rays (various forms of radiation) into space. When these charged particles arrive at Earth, they may get trapped in Earth's magnetic field and excite molecules of gas in our atmosphere.

These molecules can light up the regions near the North and South Poles of the planet, where the magnetic field lines disappear into Earth. This light, which appears to move and flicker, can be stunningly beautiful. It is generally known as an **aurora.** In the north, an aurora is called the aurora borealis or **northern lights.** In the south, it's called the aurora australis or **southern lights.**

Sunspots follow an 11-year cycle. The beginning of the cycle is marked by few sunspots, and toward the end, there are many sunspots. At the peak of the sunspot cycle, new sunspots appear on the Sun's surface every day. Interestingly, some scientists suspect that increased sunspot activity is linked with warmer temperatures on Earth.

OBSERVE SUNSPOTS SAFELY

Never try to observe sunspots directly. Instead, use the Sun's reflection on a piece of poster board. Here's how:

WHAT YOU NEED   small Plexiglas mirror
large sheet of white poster board
helper

When the Sun is low on the horizon, capture the Sun's reflection in the mirror and aim it toward the poster board, which a helper holds a footstep or two away. The image of the Sun and its sunspots will appear on the board. Swap places so the helper can see the sunspots, too.

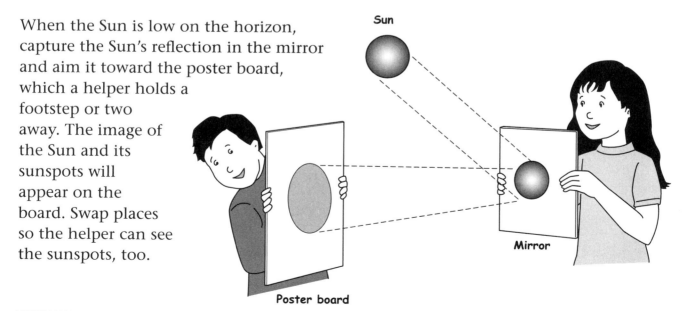

Sun

Mirror

Poster board

Solar Hiccups

Hiccups from the Sun? Well, sort of. Massive solar flares called **coronal mass ejections** aren't really hiccups, but they can wreak havoc here on Earth.

A coronal mass ejection is a massive bubble of gas that periodically erupts from the Sun and discharges a wave of charged particles toward Earth. When these particles arrive at Earth, they don't just produce auroras. They can disrupt functioning of artificial **satellites** (objects orbiting a celestial body such as Earth) and even cause blackouts of entire cities.

Because these eruptions cause so much trouble, scientists are always closely monitoring the Sun. Luckily, they can predict when the Sun's hiccups will occur. They simply watch for an S-shaped formation of plasma called a **sigmoid** to appear on the surface of the Sun. Every time one of these appears, look out! A wave of power failures may be on the way.

SHOW WHAT LIFE WOULD LOOK LIKE IF THE SUN WERE FARTHER AWAY OR CLOSER TO US

The Sun provides us with just the right amount of warmth and light to thrive. But the Sun does much more. It generates our weather and wind and feeds plants through the process of photosynthesis. The plants in turn produce oxygen for us to breathe.

WHAT YOU NEED   crayons or markers and paper
cardboard box

1 Draw a picture to show how different life-forms might look if our Sun were farther away. Draw another picture to show how plants and animals might look if the Sun were much closer. What adaptations would living creatures need to survive?

2 Place the cardboard box over a small patch of grass in your backyard. Lift the box and check the color of the grass each day. What happens to the grass without sunshine? What do you

think would happen if you watered and fertilized the grass as usual, but left the box over the grass for more than a month?

Origin of the Sun

Scientists think the Sun formed around 5 billion years ago from immense clouds of gas and dust pulled together by the forces of gravity. Over time, this mass compacted and squished together. And then it compacted and squished together some more. Eventually all of the squishing and compacting created heat and pressure powerful enough to trigger massive internal explosions. These explosions are known as **nuclear reactions.** They are the producers of the Sun's perpetual energy.

As you might imagine, explosions that never end create blistering heat. The Sun's surface is a broiling 12,000°F (7,000°C), more than hot enough to melt steel. Yet that's downright cold compared to the Sun's core, where temperatures as high as 28 million°F (16 million°C) are generated.

A 1-mile (1.6-km)–wide cube of the Sun's interior could easily boil all of the oceans of Earth.

A mere pinhead of matter from the Sun's core would kill you, even if you were standing 100 miles (160 km) away.

Crank up that air conditioner and get me some more ice!

The amount of energy produced by the Sun staggers the imagination. To generate just five minutes' worth of heat and light, the Sun must convert 120 billion tons (109 billion t) of hydrogen into helium. Just 1 pound (0.5 kg) of hydrogen converted in this way produces the equivalent energy of 10 tons (9.0719 t) of coal. Very efficient.

With its "thermostat" set so high, the Sun might be expected to burn itself out quickly, right? Not exactly. Scientists estimate that Sol has enough nuclear fuel to keep creating energy for at least another 5 billion years.

What is the solar system?

Our solar system is comprised of the Sun and all of the celestial objects that revolve around it. That includes the nine planets and their moons, plus all of the asteroids, comets, meteoroids, dust, and so on. There are probably millions of similar solar systems throughout the universe.

Although we know today that Earth and all of the planets orbit the Sun, people once believed that everything, including the Sun, revolved around Earth. This was called the **geocentric** model of the solar system.

In 1543 an astronomer named Nicholas Copernicus (1473–1543) first proposed in a book the **heliocentric,** or Sun-centered, model. The public promptly rejected his model. And because his views went against the religious belief that Earth was the center of everything, the Roman Catholic Church banned the book for over 200 years.

When in 1632 another astronomer, Galileo Galilei (1564–1642), tried to defend the Copernican model of the solar system, the Catholic Church convicted him of heresy (giving an opinion that goes against the teaching of the church). As punishment, he was sentenced to house arrest for life. Although he continued his studies, he wasn't allowed to publish any of his findings.

Centuries later, in 1992, the Catholic Church issued a formal apology to Galileo. Interestingly, according to polls, at least one-third of Earth's population still falsely believe that the Sun revolves around Earth.

What's the solar wind?

The **solar wind** is nothing like the wind we feel here on Earth. It is neither air nor gas but a flow of an electrically charged gaslike substance called **plasma,** emitted from the Sun's outermost atmosphere. The solar wind flows throughout our solar system and beyond.

Scientists are currently working on a new generation of space-ships that will one day be powered by this wind. Like the *Niña,* the *Pinta,* and the *Santa Maria* in Columbus's day, these new ships will be equipped not with gas-powered rockets but with huge sails. The sails, made of an extremely thin plastic and measuring miles (kilometers) across, wouldn't be propelled by gusts of air or gas. Rather they would convert the solar wind's charged particles to a limitless power source.

What's a cosmic year?

A **cosmic year** is the time it takes our Sun to travel around the center of our **galaxy** (a conglomeration of billions or trillions of stars), the **Milky Way.** Moving at a speed of 135 miles (217 km) per second, that journey takes roughly 225 million years.

The last time our solar system was in its present location in the galaxy was when the dinosaurs had just begun to appear.

SHOW WHEN THE SUN IS CLOSEST TO EARTH

Do you think the Sun is closer to Earth in summer or in winter? Believe it or not, it's farther away from us when it's summer in the northern hemisphere. We feel more warmth in summer because the northern hemisphere of Earth is tilted toward the Sun, so that we receive more direct sunlight. In winter, the northern hemisphere of Earth is tilted away from the Sun, so we get less direct sunlight.

Of course, just the opposite is true in the southern hemisphere, where Australia and South America are located. Our summer, in fact, is their winter and our winter is their summer.

WHAT YOU NEED
softball
marker
flashlight

1 Take the softball and make a small mark about one-quarter the distance from the top.

2 Hold the ball next to the flashlight and watch where the lamp's light falls when you rotate the ball back slightly. You can see that when the ball is tilted the right way, the mark is located farther away from the lamp and receives light at a glancing angle.

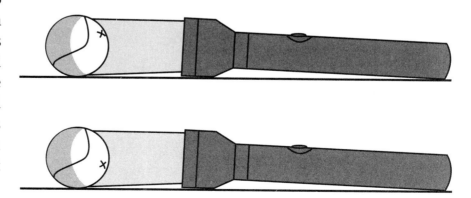

3 Rotate the ball slightly forward again, and the mark moves closer and receives light more directly. This is what happens with Earth when it's tilted different ways in relation to the Sun.

What's a solar eclipse?

A solar eclipse occurs when the new Moon passes in perfect alignment between Earth and the Sun and blocks out either all or part of the Sun for a few moments. Most new Moons pass just slightly above or below the Sun, so that an eclipse does not occur. Sometimes the Moon passes partially over the Sun and only part of the Sun is blocked from view. This is a *partial eclipse*.

Total eclipses are rare and can only be seen from small portions of Earth at a time. That's why scientists have to travel all over the world to observe them. Scientists can gather new information about the Sun when its brightest portion is covered by the Moon. It's a great time, for example, to study the Sun's corona, or outer atmosphere.

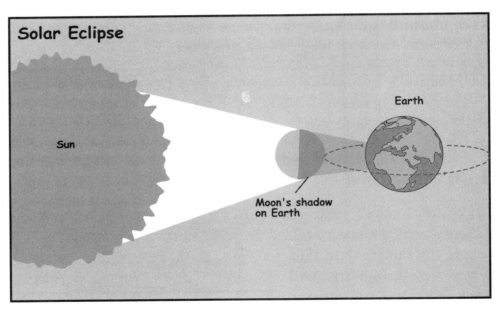

Solar Eclipse

Sun

Earth

Moon's shadow
on Earth

Viewing a solar eclipse is an unforgettable experience. As the Sun's light is increasingly blocked by the Moon, your surroundings grow dark and may even take on strange colors. The brighter stars and planets may also be visible in the daytime sky, although very briefly. When the Sun is almost completely blocked, it takes on the appearance of a giant ring.

FAST FACTS about the SUN

Diameter: 865,000 miles (1,392,000 km).

Temperature: 12,000°F (7,000°C) at surface, 28 million°F (16 million°C) at the core.

Weight of Sunlight: As strange as it sounds, all light has weight. Every square mile of sunlight weighs 3 pounds (1.36 kg/km²). If you could weigh all of the sunbeams striking Earth at this moment, they would tip the scales at 87,700 tons (78,930 t).

Gravity: A person would weigh 28 times more on the Sun than on Earth.

Why the Sun Turns Red at Sunset: Actually, the Sun does not turn red at all. One of the reasons it appears that way is that there is dust in Earth's atmosphere. The more dust that gets into the air during the day, the more the Sun will look red when it sets. This is because we are looking through the dust. The most spectacular sunsets often happen after a volcano has erupted, because volcanoes belch huge masses of grit into the atmosphere.

Why Sunbeams Don't Always Travel in a Straight Line: When you see the Sun set, you are actually seeing bent, or refracted, light. The setting Sun is really an illusion caused by the bending of light in Earth's atmosphere. The moment you see its image touch the ground, the real Sun has already dropped completely below the horizon. (See the activity "See How Light Is Bent.")

Energy Production: The Sun generates its immense energy through an endless chain of nuclear explosions. The massive gravity forces in the Sun's core heat hydrogen gas to a point where the gas's atoms fuse, creating helium and a burst of heat. The Sun gives off an estimated 40,000 watts of light from every square inch (6.45 W/cm²) of its surface.

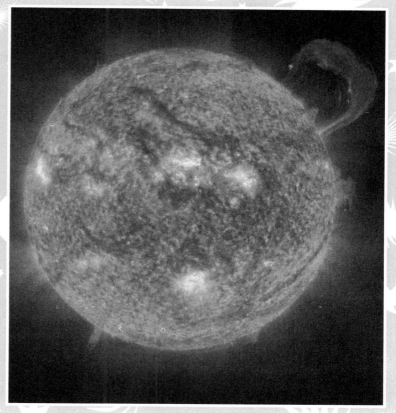

Rotation: The Sun rotates from west to east, in the same direction the planets travel around it. Because the Sun is not solid but gaseous, parts of it rotate at different speeds. The Sun's equator, an imaginary east–west line around its center, rotates completely around in about 25 days. Its poles, by contrast, take more than 30 days.

SHOW HOW LIGHT IS BENT

You can see how light is bent, or refracted.

WHAT YOU NEED   clear glass

water

spoon

Fill the glass about half full with water and place the spoon in the water. If you look at the spoon sideways at the waterline, you'll notice that the top and bottom halves do not join up. The spoon appears to be bent. Light is being refracted. This is the same thing that happens when the Sun or Moon is near Earth's horizon.

When the Sun Dies

When a star's hydrogen fuel runs low, it begins processing its helium fuel, which is less efficient. When the star can no longer work efficiently, its temperature drops. Thus begins its long road toward death. But with 5 billion years' worth of hydrogen fuel remaining, our own Sun has a long way to go to exhaust its supply.

What will happen when the end finally does come? Eventually the Sun will process all of that secondary fuel—its helium—and, instead of shrinking, it will expand—to 10 times its normal size. This bloated giant's diameter may grow as great as 97 million miles (156,106,368 km).

Because Earth is only 93 million miles from the Sun, this would mean that our planet would be swallowed up by the expanding Sun.

What's left of the Sun's atmosphere would then gradually drift off, leaving a shrunken core called a **white dwarf.** This white dwarf Sun would then spend the rest of its life cooling off—a process that takes about a trillion years.

• • •

Phew! Our spaceship is overheating. Unless we want to be slowly steamed like sardines in a can, we'd better take off. Let's move on to a quick tour of the solar system, starting from the closest planet to the Sun to the one that's farthest away. Ready? Hang on. Retro rockets firing!

SHOW HOW PLANETS AND STARS ARE FORMED

A 10-second demonstration illustrates nicely how planets and stars form from dust and debris in space.

WHAT YOU NEED   shaker of black pepper

bowl of water

spoon

Shake the pepper (give it a good six or seven shakes) into the water. The pepper will spread out on the water's surface. Now take the spoon and stir the water until a little whirlpool has formed. Stop and watch what happens.

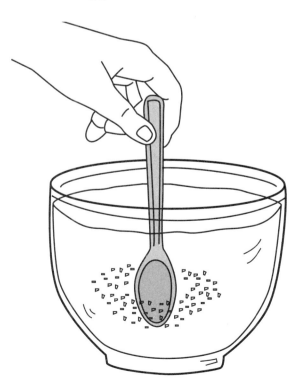

See the "planet" forming at the bottom of the bowl? This is how gravity works in space. Matter and debris are pulled in toward each other until a clump is formed. The clump tightens, becomes more dense, and grows over millions of years. *Voilà!* A pepper planet!

Whether a clump eventually becomes a star or a planet depends on various factors, the most important of which are size and density. If Jupiter, for example, had grown between 50 and 100 times more massive, it may have produced enough internal pressure and heat to flare into a Sun. Can you imagine what our sunrises would look like with not one but *two* Suns in the sky?

Planets, Asteroids, Comets, and Meteors

As we back away from the Sun, you may notice through the glare a very small, very fast-moving, crater-pocked globe. This is the planet Mercury.

Mercury

Of all the planets, Mercury orbits the closest to the Sun, at an average distance of 36 million miles (58 million km). Its proximity (nearness) to the Sun can be compared to the proximity of a hamburger to the hot coals on a grill. Yes, it's *hot* here.

FAST FACTS about MERCURY

Average Distance from the Sun: 36 million miles (58 million km).

Diameter: 3,032 miles (4,880 km).

Day: 59 Earth days.

Year: 88 Earth days.

Surface Temperature: −270°F (−173°C) to 800°F (427°C).

Visits from Spacecraft: Only one spacecraft from Earth has come close to Mercury: the *Mariner 10* flew by in 1974 and again in 1975.

During Mercury's very long day (it takes the equivalent of 59 Earth days to make one rotation), temperatures can soar to 800°F (427°C). But things cool off in a hurry when the planet turns away from the Sun and night falls. Then the temperature can plummet to −270°F (−173°C).

Roughly one-third the size of Earth, Mercury takes just 88 Earth days to orbit the Sun. In fact, the planet is named for its speedy orbit. In Roman mythology, Mercury was the swift messenger who wore the winged sandals.

Mercury's short years and long period of rotation mean that it experiences only three of its days over a period of two of its years.

Observing Mercury

It's not easy to see Mercury from Earth because it orbits so close to the Sun. Periodically it makes appearances very low on the horizon about an hour before sunrise and an hour after sunset. It is a safe bet that most people have never laid eyes on this elusive world, or if they have, they never realized what it was.

BUILD YOUR OWN ROCKET

You can build your own rocket ship that really lifts off with some very simple materials. For the highest flight, keep your materials as light as possible.

WHAT YOU NEED
    paper (Typing or computer paper is fine.)

    scissors

    transparent tape

    plastic 35-mm film canister (The cap must fit inside the rim, not outside. Ask for empties at a photo shop.)

    antacid tablet (Alka-Seltzer or any one that fizzes)

    safety glasses or glasses

    water

    adult helper

1 To make the rocket body, roll up the sheet of paper and tape it along the edge. Cut out shapes for the nose cone and fins, as illustrated. The body may be short or long.

2 Place the lid end of the canister *down*.

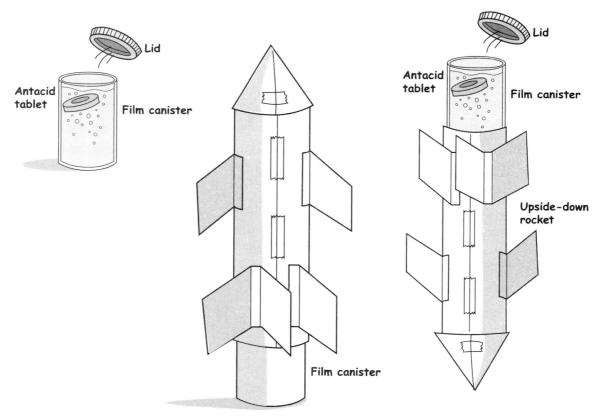

3 Tape the canister to one edge of paper. Roll the paper around the canister, and tape it again.

4 Tape the fins to the body.

5 Roll and tape the nose cone together and tape it to the top of the body.

6 Put on your glasses.

7 Turn your rocket upside down and open the canister lid. Fill the canister one-third full with water.

8 Take the rocket outdoors, and be ready to launch, with everyone clear, before you go on to the next step.

9 Working very quickly, have an adult drop half of the fizzy antacid tablet into the canister and snap the lid shut fast. Stand the rocket on a driveway or sidewalk and stand back!

How does it work? As the antacid tablet dissolves in the water, it creates a gas. This is what makes the water fizz. The escaping gas expands in the canister until it blows the lid off, providing the thrust needed to lift your rocket off the ground.

Source: Idea courtesy NASA. See jpl.nasa.gov./

Venus

From Earth it looks like the brightest star in the sky. But it's not really a star. And when we peer at it through a telescope, its surface utterly fails to **resolve** (become visible or distinct). We see a bright, glowing disk and no more. This world, we discover, is mysteriously shrouded in a permanent cloud cover.

Venus, named for the Roman goddess of love and beauty, is the second planet from the Sun and usually the closest planet to Earth.

Unlike Mercury, Venus has probably been seen by virtually everyone. That's because it frequently sets shortly after the Sun in the evening sky or rises early in the morning just before the Sun and glows like a beacon. It is so bright, in fact, that it is often reported as a UFO.

Although Venus is significantly farther away from the Sun than Mercury, its surface is actually hotter. How is that possible?

The greenhouse effect.

The **greenhouse effect** is what happens when a permanent cloud or gas cover traps the Sun's heat and prevents it from escaping into space. The gas acts like the glass in a greenhouse on Earth. In Venus's case, the gas cover is made of carbon dioxide. Carbon dioxide is an especially effective gas for trapping heat.

Could the greenhouse effect that makes Venus so hot happen on Earth?

Scientists give a disturbing answer: possibly. Our burning of fossil fuels (oil, gas, and coal) creates increased carbon dioxide in the atmosphere, which, just as on Venus, traps sunlight and heat. If we continue to pollute the atmosphere as we're doing now, Earth may continue to grow warmer.

Your family can help prevent the greenhouse effect on Earth by walking more and driving less. Can you think of any other ways?

CREATE YOUR OWN GREENHOUSE EFFECT

You can see for yourself how the greenhouse effect works in your own backyard.

WHAT YOU NEED   2 cardboard boxes (or large bowls)

transparent tape

2 bulb-type thermometers

plastic wrap

1 Take the two boxes and place them outdoors in the Sun.

2 Leave the tops open and tape a thermometer in each box.

3 Cover the top of one box securely with plastic wrap.

4 After an hour in the Sun, check both thermometers. Which box is hotter, the open one or the one covered in plastic wrap?

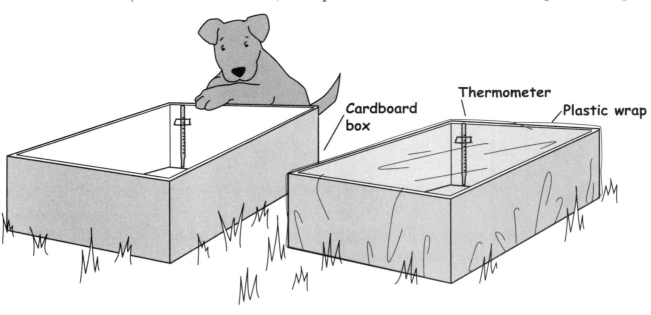

Thermometer

Cardboard box

Plastic wrap

As our spaceship breaks through this superdense cloud cover, we finally get a glimpse of the Venusian surface. It's not a pretty sight. Burned-out lava plains, festering volcanoes, and great yawning craters. The famous Mead Crater here is 174 miles (280 km) wide.

Although more than 20 unmanned spacecraft have visited Venus, it is a safe bet that humans will never set foot on its terrain. Not only would they be baked alive in temperatures hot enough to melt lead (900°F, 482°C), they would also be crushed to death. To stand in the Venusian atmosphere is the equivalent of standing under about .62 mile (1 km) of water. The pressure, in fact, is about 90 times that on the surface of Earth. Humans simply cannot survive in such conditions.

Because they're nearly identical in size, Venus and Earth are sometimes called sisters. But there is really little family resemblance. Let's consider the contrasts.

Ours is a breathtakingly beautiful blue world covered by seas, lakes, and rivers. The oceans of Venus, if it ever had them, were boiled away long ago.

Earth's atmosphere draws moisture from the surfaces of its oceans and lakes and transports it via clouds over a broad area. Eventually, nearly every area that needs rain gets it through this miraculous transport system. The Venusian atmosphere holds a permanent cloud cover saturated not with sweet water but with sulfuric acid. This poisonous cloud never clears to let the Sun shine through. It envelops Venus in a perpetual gloom.

Earth wears a lush coat of plant life, which produces oxygen for millions of different types of animals to breathe. You can't breathe on Venus. You'd be instantly suffocated by the carbon dioxide and other poisonous gases. There is no life there.

If all this weren't nightmarish enough, consider the length of the Venusian day. It takes Venus the equivalent of 243 Earth days just to spin around once. What this astonishingly slow rotation means is that a Venusian day is actually longer than a Venusian year. A year is the time it takes a planet to go around the Sun one time. It takes Venus 224.7 days.

The Shape of Orbits

All of the planets follow elliptical, or egg-shaped, not circular, paths around the Sun. Venus's orbit is the closest to a circle, while Pluto's is the most eccentric. Eccentricity is a measure of the amount the orbit varies from a circle.

FAST FACTS about VENUS

Average Distance from the Sun: 67 million miles (108 million km).

Diameter: 7,520 miles (12,103 km).

Day: 243 Earth days.

Year: 224.7 Earth days.

Surface Temperature: 900°F (482°C).

Average Distance from Earth: Venus is the planet that comes closest to Earth. At its closest approach, it is a mere 26 million miles (42 million km) away. Still, that's more than 100 times farther away from us than the Moon.

Oceans: Scientists once thought Venus was covered in an ocean of petroleum or oil. Others pooh-poohed that idea and claimed the planet was covered in seltzer water! In fact, it has no ocean, although it may have had water millions of years ago.

Rotation: On Venus, the Sun rises in the west and sets in the east. That's just the opposite of what we experience on Earth. In fact, Venus is the only planet to have this kind of reversed (called retrograde) motion. Why? Scientists think that early in its history, Venus was probably struck by a very large object. The impact of this object was so powerful that it actually stopped Venus from spinning and forced it to rotate in the opposite way.

Storms: Venus is constantly zapped with severe lightning storms. As the Soviet space probe *Venera 12* made its descent through the planet's atmosphere in 1978, it detected 1,000 lightning flashes in only a 4-mile (6.4-km) area.

Acid Rain: The concentrated sulfuric acid in the Venusian cloud cover may occasionally mix with other acids and form "raindrops" corrosive enough to dissolve lead and tin and burn away human flesh in minutes.

FIND VENUS IN THE DAYTIME

Venus is so bright, it can sometimes be seen in the daytime.

WHAT YOU NEED   current astronomical chart
piece of cardboard

Consult the astronomical chart to see when Venus will appear in the evening or early morning sky. When the sky is crystal clear (no clouds or moisture in the air), look to the east of the setting Sun or, when Venus appears in the morning, to the west of the rising Sun. Block the Sun from your eyesight with the piece of cardboard or a portion of a building. Use care not to look directly at the Sun.

Mars

Our spaceship will skip around the third planet from the Sun, Earth, in order to get to the fourth, Mars. Named for the Roman god of war, Mars is one of the brightest, and certainly reddest, objects in the sky.

Unlike Venus, Mars has no permanent cloud cover to veil its face from us. It's the only planet that allows us to see its surface so clearly from Earth. And that's lucky because Mars boasts some of the most interesting terrain in the solar system.

Through a moderately powered telescope, you can sometimes see the polar ice caps at the north or south poles of the planet. If you observe them through the very long Martian seasons of winter and summer, they appear to grow and shrink. (But sometimes in Martian summer they're too small to be seen from Earth.)

Mysterious dark areas appear to slowly shift position across the planet's surface. These shifts are due to light-colored sands being blown across darker ground areas. Earth-based observers may not always be able to see this kind of detail. Winds on Mars can exceed speeds of 250 miles (400 km) per hour. Sometimes dust storms grow large enough to obscure the entire planet. When this happens, few or no surface details can be seen and Mars becomes a frustrating target for your telescope.

Approaching in our spaceship, we encounter two small, potato-shaped moons roughly the size of cities. These are called Deimos and Phobos. By a bizarre coincidence, Jonathan Swift's book *Gulliver's Travels,* written in 1726, describes these two moons of Mars 151 years before they were actually discovered.

From the orbits of either of these moons, we can easily make out the craters of Mars. One of these craters is the biggest in the entire solar system: Hellas. Located in the southern hemisphere, Hellas is over 1,000 miles (1,600

Viewing Mars through a Telescope or Binoculars

The best time to see Mars through a telescope is when it is closest to Earth. It swings close to Earth roughly every two years. Mars's close approaches can be viewed two months before to two months after these peak months:

August 2003	May 2016
November 2005	July 2018
December 2007	October 2020
January 2010	December 2022
March 2012	January 2025
April 2014	February 2027

km) wide and is deeper than Mount Everest is high. Scientists speculate that the asteroid that made the crater must have been at least 100 miles (161 km) across.

Mars also has a gargantuan volcano called Olympus Mons. The largest volcano ever seen anywhere, it's about 15 miles (24 km) high, three times higher than Mount Everest.

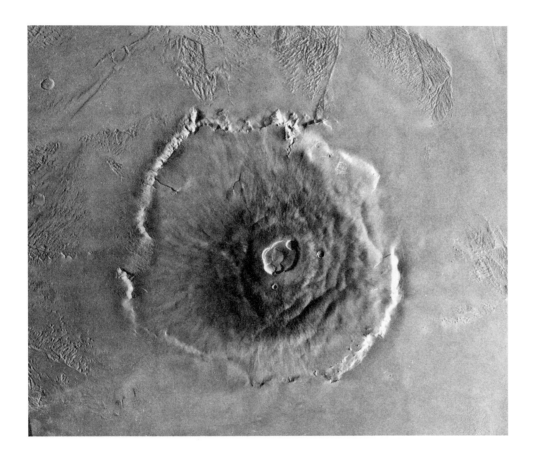

In the northern hemisphere, there is yet another impressive site. Here, a massive basin descends 6 miles (9.6 km) below the average elevation. The basin is remarkably smooth and featureless. It looks as if it had been polished smooth by a large body of water, and may be evidence of a past ocean.

Today the basin is bone dry, of course, and Mars has no surface water anywhere. Yet there is water on Mars. Scientists believe some water lies trapped at the north and south poles as ice.

Due to all the dust that often blows up into the atmosphere, Mars usually has a brownish yellow sky, but it appears dark blue when conditions are clear. Its terrain is rock-strewn and desertlike with reddish orange dirt that looks like rust. In fact, much of it is just that: rust. If the dirt here is rusty, you may be able to guess which metal element is present in abundance. (Iron.)

While areas at the equator sometimes reach 70°F (21.1°C) during the day, the temperature plummets when night falls, reaching –100°F (–73°C) or more. The thin atmosphere here is simply incapable of holding heat. The thin air also makes it impossible for any greenhouse effect, as that found on Venus, to take place. The atmosphere is made up almost entirely of carbon dioxide, the gas we exhale.

Is There Life on Mars?

A century ago some astronomers were convinced that Mars was inhabited by highly intelligent beings. As one scientist, Percival Lowell (1855–1916), peered through his telescope, he was certain he saw canals all over the surface of the planet. The canals, he said, must have been built by Martians for transporting water long distances between cities. Even though he persuaded a lot of people to believe what he was seeing, the "canals" were later proven to be only optical illusions.

Mars does have canal-like channels, but they neither carry nor hold water. Nor can they be seen from Earth. However, they may have held water in the planet's distant past. And scientists believe if there were water on Mars, there may also have been some form of life.

In the 1970s, two U.S. space probes called *Viking 1* and *Viking 2* touched down on Mars specifically looking for those signs of life. Neither found any. The *Pathfinder* probe in 1997 also found no obvious signs of living organisms.

End of story? Not quite. Scientists studying meteorites from Mars in 1996 found something amazing: tiny fossilized bacteria— or at least they looked like fossilized bacteria. The extremely rare meteorites containing the bacteria are thought to have been blown off Mars in a cosmic collision billions of years ago. Eventually they fell to Earth. (Scientists are able to identify these meteorites as having come from Mars by analyzing certain elements and gases inside them. Of the more than 20,000 meteorites collected by scientists on Earth, only 13 of them are thought to have come from Mars.) The fossils inside these ancient rocks, some say, are proof life once existed on Mars.

FAST FACTS about MARS

Average Distance from Sun: 141.6 million miles (227.9 million km).

Diameter: 4,222 miles (6,794 km).

Day: Although Mars is only about half the size of Earth, its day (the time it takes the planet to rotate once) is 24 hours, 37 minutes, almost identical to that of Earth.

Year: 687 Earth days.

Surface Temperature: In most areas on Mars, daytime temperatures rarely go above −20°F (−29°C), although they can get to at least 20°F (−6°C). Nighttime temperatures plummet to below −143°F (−97°C).

Biggest Canyon: Among the most impressive surface features on Mars is a 2,000-mile (3,220-km)–long canyon called Valle Marineris. It is 3 times as deep and 26 times as long as Earth's Grand Canyon.

Ice Caps: The polar ice caps are mostly made not of water but of frozen carbon dioxide, otherwise known as "dry ice." The ice caps on Mars alternately grow and shrink with the planet's seasons.

"Face" on Mars: The famous rock "face" on Mars, as seen in the tabloids and in the movie *Mission to Mars,* was not made by Martians. First photographed by the Viking Orbiter in 1976, the "face" is actually a mountain. Its humanlike features are due to a combination

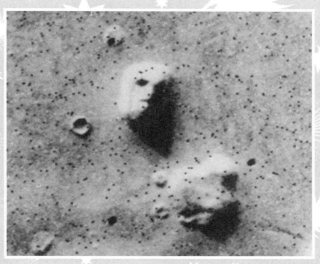

of factors: missing photographic data called "bit errors" (photo transmissions must travel a long way from Mars to Earth, and parts of the information can become lost) and sunlight striking the rock at just the right angle. People have also seen hearts and smiley faces in photos of Mars, due to similar explainable phenomena. In 2001, the Mars Orbital Camera took a higher-resolution photo of this feature that clearly shows that the object is just a regular old mountain.

Humans on Mars: Missions to Mars with unmanned probes are ongoing. A human mission to Mars is possible in the future. In fact, scientists believe it will happen within the next 20 years.

Other scientists, however, are not so sure. They argue that the bacteria may have crawled onto or formed on the meteorites after they landed on Earth. Scientists all over the world are still hotly debating these intriguing finds.

Meanwhile, one scientist, Timothy Kral at the University of Arkansas, has found a certain type of bacteria that is quite capable of surviving in conditions almost exactly like those on Mars. These bacteria, called methanogens, thrive without oxygen in a bath of carbon dioxide and hydrogen gases. "If man were to go to Mars someday and introduce life," Kral says, "this might be the form of life that would grow there." Where are methanogens found on Earth? Only inside the stomachs of cows.

Find Out More

Now that you know the truth about Mars, it's fun to look at some fictional versions. Two of the greatest science fiction stories of all time about Mars are *The Martian Chronicles* (Earth astronauts visiting a Mars richly and poetically populated with weird aliens and ghosts), by Ray Bradbury, and *The War of the Worlds* (Martians invading Earth), by H. G. Wells. You can find them in your local library.

If your local video store carries old classics, you may be able to find *The Angry Red Planet* (1959). All of the Martian scenes and creatures were shot through a red lens, a supercheap special effect that created an astonishingly atmospheric sense of otherworldliness. Just don't listen too closely to the shlocky dialogue.

Wells's *War of the Worlds* was also made into a movie, as well as a live radio show. On October 30, 1938, the radio play was presented as a live news broadcast which convinced some listeners that America was being attacked—for real—by Martian invaders.

The Asteroid Belt

As our spaceship leaves Mars and heads for Jupiter, we must take care to avoid hitting an asteroid. An **asteroid** is a giant chunk of rock drifting around in space. There are millions of these floating

about. Scientists think they're leftover debris from planetary collisions early in our solar system's formation. (Want to see what a typical asteroid looks like? Just bake a potato and pock its surface with small crater marks.) Asteroids are sometimes classified as minor planets.

Many asteroids orbit the Sun in a swarm or belt, called the **asteroid belt,** between Mars and Jupiter. Scientists know of approximately 100,000 asteroids in this area that measure from less than 0.62 mile (1 km) to 600 miles (1,000 km) across (roughly the size of a small state).

Although one out of every five asteroids is discovered by backyard astronomers, asteroids are difficult to see from Earth. However, occasionally one leaves its orbit and comes close to us.

In May 1999, astronomers made a stunning calculation: in the year 2027, a 0.5-mile (.804-km)–wide asteroid named 1999AN10 is going to come very close to colliding with Earth. They've even figured out the exact day the asteroid will make its close pass: August 7.

What's the Difference?

meteor a rock fragment from space and the streak of light it makes as it enters Earth's atmosphere and burns up. It is mistakenly referred to as a **shooting star.**

meteorite a rock fragment from space that survives the plummet through Earth's atmosphere and actually hits Earth.

meteoroid any solid body smaller than an asteroid traveling through space.

asteroid any very large meteoroid.

planetesimal any one of billions of orbiting bodies (asteroids) or debris that massed together to form the planets.

comet a large ball of ice, dust, and gas in space.

FIGURE IT OUT

Scientists are already considering developing missiles that would blow up incoming asteroids or at least alter their course. Figure out some other ways humans could prevent asteroids from striking Earth. How could we protect ourselves from an impact?

How close will the asteroid come? NASA's Near Earth Object tracking office says it could be as close as 19,000 miles (30,400 km). This probably doesn't seem very close to you, but in terms of near collisions in space, that is quite close. Approaching to within one-twelfth the distance to the Moon, the asteroid will be visible to observers on Earth without the aid of telescopes or binoculars. It will appear, in fact, as a moderately bright star.

Scientists are certain the asteroid will not strike Earth, and they say the closest approach could be thousands of miles farther off.

Dinosaur Disaster

The extinction of the dinosaurs is thought to have been caused by the fallout from an asteroid collision. The evidence is a 100-mile (160-km)–wide crater (now buried under sedimentary rock) in the Yucatán Peninsula, and a second crater, about three times as large, under the Arabian Sea off India. The Yucatán crater was dug out by an asteroid 10 miles (16.09 km) wide. The Arabian Sea crater was blasted by an asteroid 25 miles (40 km) wide. Both asteroids collided into Earth at the time of the dinosaurs' extinction, 65 million years ago.

Besides the craters, other evidence of the bombardment includes a layer of an element called iridium, which is deposited by asteroids on impact. This layer is in soil dating from 65 million years ago and is found around the world. Its presence indicates that a massive impact did indeed occur around the time of the dinosaurs' demise.

Asteroids are responsible for mass extinctions even earlier in Earth's history. In fact, the dinosaurs may have appeared as a result of a similar asteroid crash 251 million years ago. In this disaster, possibly the worst ever, scientists calculate that enough lava poured out of Earth to cover the planet in a layer of lava 10 feet (3 m) deep. The oceans also dropped a whopping 820 feet (250 m). Most devastating was the loss of sunlight caused by the thick clouds of smoke and debris from the blast. The Sun probably was not visible for months.

As a result, 90 percent of all sea life died, along with 70 percent of land animals and most plants. This mass die-off made way for the appearance of new plants and animals.

They also say an asteroid 0.62 mile (1 km) in size strikes Earth once every 100,000 years. Thus our odds of being hit by something big in the next century are 1 in 1,000.

Find Out More

Check out NASA's Near Earth objects web site (neo.jpl.nasa.gov).

First Asteroid Landing

If scientists can put a man on the Moon and a lander on Mars, why can't they send a probe to land on and study an asteroid? In fact, they can and they did, for the first time ever with the NEAR-Shoemaker space probe, which landed on the 21-mile (34-km)–long asteroid 433 Eros, 200 million miles (322 million km) from Earth, on February 12, 2001. The car-sized probe sent back tens of thousands of pictures that revealed a cratered, rock- and boulder-strewn terrain.

Asteroid Shaped like a What?

A dog bone the size of New Jersey is floating in space within the orbit of Jupiter. Well, not a real dog bone, but an asteroid that looks exactly like one. Scientists call this bruiser of a rock 216 Kleopatra. "There is nothing like this that we know of. It's a unique object," says Steven Ostro of NASA's Jet Propulsion Laboratory, who has studied the rock. "It's the most unusual shape that we have ever seen and it's fantastic that it exists." So far scientists have not seen any poodle-shaped asteroids to go with the state-sized bone, but stay tuned. In space, darn near anything is likely to show up sooner or later.

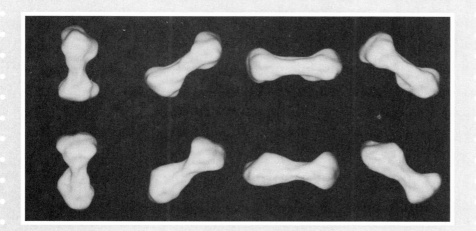

Jupiter

Leaving the orbit of Mars and the asteroid belt, we soon encounter one of the most magnificent worlds in the solar system: Jupiter.

It is perfectly sensible that Jupiter was named after the Roman king of the gods. For sheer color, size, and beauty, no other planet in the solar system strikes the eye quite like it. It is a huge world, 88,700 miles (142,800 km) in diameter. Roughly 1,300 times the volume of Earth, it is big enough to contain all of the planets in the solar system.

With at least 28 moons orbiting around it, Jupiter appears to reign over its own miniature solar system. This seems only appropriate when we consider that with more mass, Jupiter could have become a sun itself.

Unlike Mercury, Venus, Earth, and Mars, Jupiter is called a gas giant. That is, it's comprised mainly of hydrogen and helium gas, and liquids instead of solid rock. Above Jupiter's small solid core is a layer of a weird element called liquid metallic hydrogen. Above this is a layer of liquid molecular hydrogen. Above both of these layers is Jupiter's atmosphere of colorful bands of swirling hydrogen, helium, water, carbon, sulfur, neon, krypton, and xenon. Through a telescope on Earth you can see these bands move and change from night to night.

The Gas Giants

The **gas giants** (also called the Jovian planets, meaning "like Jupiter") include Jupiter, Saturn, Uranus, and Neptune. These planets are much larger and more massive than Earth and the other terrestrial (Earth-like) planets, and they are mainly composed of liquids and gases.

SHOW HOW YOUR EYES ADJUST TO THE DARK

Your eyes adjust according to how light or dark your surroundings are. In very bright conditions, the pupil of the eye shrinks to block some of the light. In very dark conditions, the pupil expands to let more light in. Nocturnal (active at night) animals often have huge eyes with very large pupils.

YOU WILL NEED   mirror

To show the pupil in action, stand in front of the mirror in a darkened room for five minutes. When you turn on the light, watch your pupils in the mirror. They will rapidly shrink.

How to Optimize Your Vision

How well your eyes resolve distant celestial objects depends on how dark your night sky is (the farther away from city lights, the better) and how much of the Moon (if any) is showing. Optimizing your vision can sometimes mean the difference between seeing the moons of Jupiter or the rings of Saturn and not seeing them at all. Here are some veteran observing tips.

1. Your eyes require at least 20 minutes to become fully adapted to the dark. The longer you sit in the dark, the larger your pupils will grow, allowing sharper night vision. The older you are, the longer it takes the eyes to adapt.

2. Stay well away from roads, not only to avoid streetlights but to prevent being "blinded" by an oncoming car's headlights. Every time you're blinded, it takes several minutes for your eyes to readapt.

3. Red light does not impair your night vision like regular white light does, so when reading sky charts, use a small, red-filtered flashlight. (You can make a red flashlight for viewing sky charts in the dark by simply taping red plastic over the lens or by lightly painting the lens red with nail polish.)

4. When possible, try to wait until an object is high in the sky before observing it. Objects high in the sky are more sharply defined than those low in the sky. That's because when you look at a celestial body just above the horizon, you have to peer through more of Earth's distorting atmosphere.

5. Extremely faint objects in the sky can sometimes be detected more with peripheral, or side, vision than with direct, or frontal, vision.

FIND JUPITER AND ITS MOONS

WHAT YOU NEED   star chart

binoculars or telescope

1 Consult the star chart to find out when Jupiter will appear in the sky. It will likely be one of the brightest celestial bodies in the sky and therefore easy to find. Peer at it through binoculars or a telescope.

2 If you're in a dark neighborhood and you look hard enough, you should be able to see tiny pinpoints of light on either side of Jupiter. These are Jupiter's largest moons. If you're lucky, you can see four of them: Io, Europa, Ganymede, and Callisto. If you're under very dark skies, try to see if you can make out any of these moons with your naked eye.

Why You'd Sound like a Munchkin on Jupiter

Because Jupiter is composed largely of two lighter-than-air gases, hydrogen and helium, your speaking voice would sound an octave or two higher than it does on Earth. Very Munchkin-like, in fact.

All sounds on Jupiter, including booming thunder, would be considerably higher pitched than they are in the thicker atmosphere of Earth.

As we view Jupiter from our spacecraft, we're struck not only by its size and fast rotation, but by its swirling bands and belts of color. We're suddenly noticing something that can't be seen from Earth. It's something astronomers never even knew existed until the *Voyager 1* spacecraft flew by in 1979: a ring.

Although it pales in comparison to the magnificent rings of Saturn, the ring of Jupiter looks something like a halo. The "halo" is composed of fine dust and rock particles.

More obvious from Earth are Jupiter's monstrous storms, some of them as large as all of North America. Jupiter's famous **Great Red Spot** is actually a perpetual storm as big as three Earths combined. Winds at speeds of 250 miles (402 km) per hour are constantly blowing around the spot.

Because of its huge mass, Jupiter sucks our spaceship toward it more powerfully than does any other planet. To blast off from its surface and escape its grip, our rocket must travel at least 133,000 miles (214,000 km) per hour. By contrast, a speed of just 2,500 miles (4,023 km) per hour is all that's needed to escape Pluto.

FAST FACTS about JUPITER

Average Distance from the Sun: 484 million miles (780 million km).

Diameter: 88,700 miles (142,800 km).

Day: For such a large planet, Jupiter spins around remarkably fast. Its day is only 9 hours and 50 minutes long.

Year: 11.9 Earth years.

Atmospheric Temperature: From about −225°F (−143°C) at the cloud tops to at least 305°F (152°C) at the lower reaches of the atmosphere.

Space Probes: Several spacecraft have visited Jupiter, starting with *Pioneer 10* in 1973.

In 1995, a tiny space probe the size of a barbecue grill was launched from the spacecraft *Galileo* and descended several miles into Jupiter's atmosphere. It managed to take numerous detailed readings until, 57 minutes later, it was completely vaporized by extreme atmospheric pressures and temperatures reaching twice the surface temperature of the Sun.

Moon Oceans: The spacecraft *Galileo* detected evidence of oceans lying under a crust of ice on two of Jupiter's moons, Europa and Callisto.

Why You'd Weigh More Than a Ton on the Sun

Jupiter is far larger than Earth and has a much greater mass. The greater a planet's mass, the greater its gravity. If you weigh 100 pounds (45.3 kg) on Earth, you would weigh 254 (115.2 kg) pounds on Jupiter. The Sun has an even greater mass. If you weigh 100 pounds (45.3 kg) on Earth, you would weigh a whopping 2,707 pounds (1,227.8 kg) on the Sun.

Use this gravity chart to figure how much you would weigh on the other planets. Simply multiply your weight by the gravitational pull (compared to Earth) of each planet.

Planet	Gravity Compared to Earth
Mercury	0.38
Venus	0.91
Earth	1.00
Mars	0.38
Jupiter	2.54
Saturn	0.93
Uranus	0.80
Neptune	1.20
Pluto	0.06

Source: NASA.

Saturn

Named after the Roman god of agriculture, Saturn is the sixth planet from the Sun and is second in size only to Jupiter. Like Jupiter, Saturn is a gas giant. It has a small solid core covered by an inner layer of liquid metallic hydrogen and an outer layer of molecular hydrogen. Saturn also suffers its share of violent storms.

In the night sky of Earth, Saturn is a bright yellow planet that is easy to locate. Viewed through a low-powered telescope, it eclipses all other planets when it comes to pure thrill power. The reason why is simple: its rings.

If conditions are right, Saturn's magnificent rings are clearly visible through low-powered telescopes. Even as dim and tiny as they may appear, the sense of wonder they create when you see them for the first time is something you'll never forget. Although from a distance the rings look like a solid halo, they are actually composed of water ice and rock particles from pebble to boulder size.

We're wise to keep our spaceship from getting too close, not only to avoid the debris of the rings, but also to keep away from Saturn's whopping 30 moons. (If people on Earth act a little crazy on the night of a full Moon, can you imagine what could happen with 30?)

Using the Ecliptic to Find a Planet

Using the naked eye alone, how can you tell the difference between a star and a planet? One way is to locate the ecliptic.

The **ecliptic** is an imaginary line that traces the Sun's path through the sky. In northern latitudes, including the continental United States, Canada, and Europe, the ecliptic crosses the southern portion of the sky.

The Moon and the planets all appear near the ecliptic (except for Pluto) because they orbit the Sun in the same plane. If you see what looks like a bright star near the ecliptic, it may well be a planet instead.

Groups of stars resembling animals, objects, or mythological figures, and often named after these things, are called **constellations.** Twelve constellations, together known as the **zodiac,** are arranged around the ecliptic. These are Aries, Taurus, Gemini, Cancer, Leo, Virgo, Libra, Scorpius, Sagittarius, Capricorn, Aquarius, and Pisces.

FAST FACTS about SATURN

Average Distance from the Sun: 887 million miles (1,427 million km).

Diameter: 75,0000 miles (120,000 km), big enough to hold 750 Earths.

Day: 10.3 hours.

Year: 29.5 Earth years.

Space Probe: Saturn was first visited by *Pioneer 11* in 1979. *Voyager 1* and *2* followed later. *Cassini*, the biggest planetary explorer the United States has ever launched, is scheduled to arrive around Saturn in June of 2004, where it will orbit for four years.

Helicopters on Titan: *Cassini* is scheduled to launch a small probe to land on Saturn's largest moon, Titan, in November 2004. Titan, at 3,200 miles (5,150 km) in diameter, is larger than the planet Pluto. Future probes to Titan may contain small helicopters, which will be used to fly from location to location and collect data.

FIGURE IT OUT

Although it feels as if Earth is standing still, we're actually racing around the Sun and across the cosmos at breakneck speed.

At this very moment, Earth at the equator is rotating at about 1,100 miles (1,770 km) per hour. At the same time, it is orbiting around the Sun at 67,000 miles (108,000 km) per hour. Also at the same time, the Sun and the entire solar system are moving around the center of the galaxy at a speed of 486,000 miles (782,000 km) per hour.

What clues can you find in the sky to figure out that we're actually moving and moving quickly?

Uranus

Everyone has trouble pronouncing the name of this planet, which came from the Greek god of the heavens. Uranus might have been better off if astronomers had simply stuck to one of its two original names, Georgium Sidus (George's Star, after King George III of England) or Herschel, after its discoverer, William Herschel (1738–1822). Most folks, in fact, called it Herschel from the time of its discovery in 1781 until around 1850, when the name Uranus took hold with the public.

Hmm. Is it the name that's bad or is that most people simply don't know how to pronounce it correctly? The real way to pronounce Uranus is YOOR-a-nus.

Only one spacecraft has visited Uranus, *Voyager 2,* in 1986, which sent back pictures of a hauntingly beautiful blue world. As we approach Uranus in our own spacecraft, we're struck by that icy blue color. It appears to envelop the entire planet like some vast sea. Move in for a closer look, though, and we see it is not water at all. It's a layer of gas called methane.

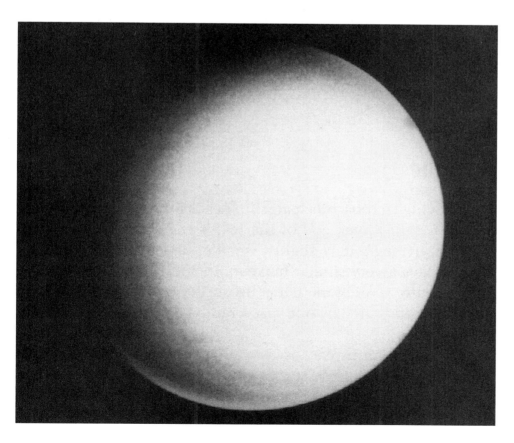

FAST FACTS about URANUS

Distance from the Sun: 1.78 billion miles (2.87 billion km).

Size: 32,300 miles (52,000 km) in diameter.

Day: 17 hours.

Year: 84 Earth years.

Moons: Most celestial bodies in our solar system are named from classical mythology. But the names of the moons of Uranus derive from the works of the English writers William Shakespeare and Alexander Pope (Juliet, Oberon, Puck, Ariel, and so on).

Methane gives the planet its uniform blue color. Yet scientists say that underneath this layer may be the same kind of belts and bands of color that appear on Jupiter.

Like Jupiter and Saturn, Uranus has a lot of moons—21 are known. It also has 11 rings composed of particles as small as dust and as large as trucks.

To find the current positions of the planets; track comets, asteroids, and satellites; and print out sky maps, check out Your Sky Online Planetarium at www.fourmilab.ch/yoursky/.

Neptune

After leaving Uranus, our spaceship heads for Neptune. Neptune, named for the Greek god of the sea, is the eighth planet from the Sun. Though it is slightly smaller than Uranus, the two planets have a very similar makeup, including the same beautiful blue outer layer of methane. Because Neptune is so distant, it has only been visited by one spacecraft—*Voyager 2,* on August 25, 1989.

Although Uranus can occasionally be seen under very dark skies, Neptune cannot be seen with the naked eye at all. Through a telescope, it appears as a dim blue-green point of light. Neptune has eight known moons and a faint ring system.

Many people think Pluto is the most distant planet from the Sun. But it isn't always. Because the orbit of Pluto is so highly elliptical, Neptune is sometimes the most distant planet in the solar system. Pluto was actually closer to the Sun than Neptune from 1979 to 1999.

To illustrate how far away from the Sun Neptune is, consider the average temperature here: –370°F (–187.77°C). *Brrrrr.*

FAST FACTS *about* NEPTUNE

Distance from the Sun: 2.8 billion miles (4.5 billion km).

Diameter: 30,000 miles (48,400 km).

Day: 18 hours.

Year: 165 Earth years.

Winds: Neptune has the fastest winds ever recorded. Its atmosphere sometimes generates gusts reaching 1,250 miles (2,000 km) per hour.

Pluto

Four light-hours from Earth (a **light-year** is the distance light travels in one year: 5.88 trillion miles, 9.463 trillion km), our ship reaches the outermost planet in the solar system, Pluto. We are now so deep in space that the Sun is just a dim beacon.

Pluto holds three distinctions: it is the smallest planet; it is usually the most distant planet from the Sun; and it has never been visited by spacecraft from Earth.

Pluto is named for the Roman god of the underworld, which is appropriate because Pluto is so far from the Sun and very dark. Astronomers searched for this tiny outpost planet for years, but it wasn't actually discovered until 1930, when Clyde Tombaugh (b. 1906), a self-described "farm boy amateur astronomer without a university education," located it in a photograph.

More people fussed over the name of this tiny blob of rock and ice than that of any other planet. Among the many suggestions for names: Apollo, Atlas, Artemis, Constance, Cronus, Perseus, Tantalus, and Zymal. After all of the experts had weighed in, the problem was once again solved by an amateur. The name Pluto was suggested by an 11-year-old girl from Oxford, England.

Pluto
Hubble Space Telescope · Faint Object Camera

PRC96-09a · ST ScI OPO · March 7, 1996 · A. Stern (SwRI), M. Buie (Lowell Obs.), NASA, ESA

PICTURE THE DISTANCE FROM THE SUN TO PLUTO

Most illustrations of the solar system show the planets quite close together in orbit around the Sun. In reality, the planets are extremely far away from each other. How far? Try this activity to show what the planet distances would be if measured against a scale in which the Sun is only 2 inches (5 cm) in diameter.

WHAT YOU NEED   2-inch (5.08-cm) cardboard circle

tape measure

9 sticks

1 Go to your local athletic or football field and place the cardboard circle down on the ground. This is the Sun. Measure 7 feet (2 m) and push one stick into the ground. This is the planet Mercury.

2 Measure and mark the distances to the rest of the planets as follows:

	Scale Distance from the Sun	
	Feet	**Meters**
Venus	13	4
Earth	18	5
Mars	27	8
Jupiter	93	28
Saturn	171	52
Uranus	344	104
Neptune	539	164
Pluto	708	216

That's right. You actually need the length of over *two* footballfields to complete these measurements. If you can't find that much empty space, try taking the same measurements on a very long sidewalk. Or you can cut all the measurements exactly in half. That way, you'll need only half as much space.

3 Want to carry this exercise out one step further? Measure the distance to one of the nearest stars, Alpha Centauri, placing a stick in the ground exactly—ahem!—916 miles (1,474 km) away.

To show the distance to the center of our galaxy, mark a spot exactly 5,945,088 miles (9,567,692 km) away!

Now are you starting to see why they call it space?

This activity is even more fun if you use scale models to show the Sun and planets. If the Sun is a jumbo-sized beach ball, you could use a softball for Jupiter, a baseball for Saturn, a golf ball for Uranus and Neptune (use different colors), a marble for Earth, a pencil eraser cut in half for Venus, an unpopped popcorn kernel or peppercorn for Mars, half a candy sprinkle for Mercury, and a sand grain for Pluto. These will not be exact representations, but they do give you a pretty good idea of the differences in size of the planets and the Sun.

FAST FACTS about PLUTO

Average Distance from the Sun: 3.67 billion miles (5.9 billion km).

Diameter: 1,457 miles (2,344 km), less than one-fifth the size of Earth.

Surface Temperature: −350° to −380°F (−212° to −228°C).

Moon: Pluto has one moon, Charon (pronounced Karen)

Classification: Because of its small size and weird orbit, some scientists have argued that Pluto isn't really a planet, but simply a really big rock. Although a few astronomers like to refer to Pluto as a "trans-Neptunian object" (something that orbits beyond Neptune), Pluto is nevertheless officially classified as a planet. To complicate things further, Pluto's moon is over half the size of its host. Thus some astronomers classify them as not planet and moon but as a double planet.

Year: 250 Earth years.

Day: 6.39 Earth days.

Space Probes: A NASA space probe is scheduled to visit the planet sometime around 2016.

The Kuiper Belt

Although Pluto is the last planet we know of in our neighborhood, we're not quite out of the solar system yet. As we cruise beyond Pluto's orbit, we enter what spaceship captains everywhere would call a "navigational hazard." Orbiting the Sun in these hinterlands is the **Kuiper Belt,** a disk-shaped swarm of from 200 million to 5 billion comets, asteroids, and fragments. The debris is actually leftover material from the formation of the solar system. Some of the comets that pass by Earth originate in the Kuiper Belt.

Although 5 billion objects seems like a lot, our spaceship is actually safer than you might think. Too much space exists between the icy bodies to worry much about collisions. Interestingly, scientists say if there were a few billion more comets and asteroids here, they would eventually crash into each other and form yet another planet.

The Oort Cloud

As we rocket out of the Kuiper Belt, we encounter yet another debris field. This one serves as a marker for the end of our solar system. Located roughly 1 light-year from the Sun, or about 1,000 times farther out than the Kuiper Belt, is the Oort Cloud.

The **Oort Cloud** isn't a cloud, but an immensely vast ring of comets extending from 1 light-year from the Sun to as far as halfway to the nearest star, Proxima Centauri. The Oort Cloud is named after the Dutch astronomer Jan Oort (1900–1992), who first proposed its existence. Scientists believe that the Oort Cloud may contain as many as a trillion comets—that's much, much larger than the Kuiper Belt. No one has ever seen the comets of the Oort Cloud, but we believe it must exist because of what we have observed about comets that pass close to Earth.

As we pass some of these comets in our ship, you may be amazed by their size. Their cores may be 1 mile (1.6 km) or more in diameter. Their outer gases sometimes spread as wide as states. And when they are occasionally jolted from their orbits and approach the Sun, their tails, the illuminated dust and gases that are blown off by solar radiation and wind, can stretch for millions of miles. Comets that collided with Earth early in its history may have been responsible for filling our oceans.

Comets

When they come close enough to be seen from Earth, comets look like fuzzy stars. Their movement, in fact, may appear to be so slow that they seem fixed in the sky. Quite the contrary. Comets streak speedily around the Sun at about 150,000 miles (240,000 km) per hour in highly elliptical orbits. And they're not starlike at all.

Comets are composed of frozen water, frozen ammonia, and solid carbon dioxide, mixed with a small amount of dust and rock particles. They are sometimes called "dirty snowballs." Comets are often responsible for the debris that becomes meteors and meteorites.

Comets are made up of three parts. In addition to the very visible tail, they include the nucleus, which is the solid center or head of the comet, and the coma, the cloud of gas and dust that surrounds the nucleus.

The word *comet* comes from the Greek word for hair because the Greeks fancied that the tails looked like flowing hair.

The most interesting comet seen in recent times was Hale-Bopp, which has a nucleus or core about twice the size of Halley's famous comet. It thrilled millions of naked-eye viewers during the spring of 1997. But because of its huge orbit, it won't revisit our night skies again until the year 4300.

Strange Beliefs about Comets

Comets have long been viewed as omens, signs of good or bad luck. In A.D. 684 people blamed an epidemic of the plague on a passing comet. Before the Battle of Hastings in 1066, William the Conqueror took the appearance of Halley's comet as a sign that he would win the great battle, and he did.

People have believed all kinds of strange things about comets. Some ancient peoples thought comets carried angels through the heavens. As late as 1910, some people believed the gases in Halley's comet were poisonous and that if the comet came close enough to Earth, they could be killed. Some people actually sealed up their houses. Others bought special gas masks and consumed "anti-comet" pills.

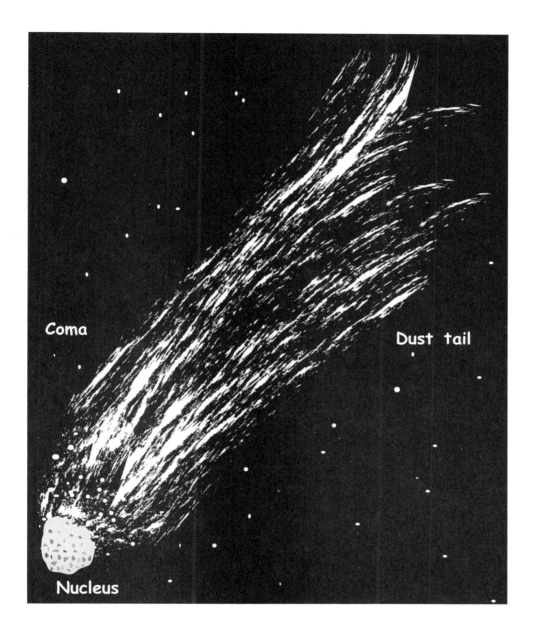

Halley's comet, which returns every 76 years, is probably the most famous of all, but not because it has been the most spectacular. So much has been written about the Comet Halley because it has been regularly seen throughout history. A comet called the Daylight comet, which last appeared just a few weeks before Halley's in 1910, was brighter than Halley's, so much so that it could even be seen in the daylight. The Daylight comet has been recorded in history only once. That's because it only returns once every 4 million years.

Meteors

Occurring several times per year, meteor showers often eclipse comets in the excitement department. Meteors rocket across the sky like fireworks. They may sometimes even smoke and boom like fireworks. Comets, by contrast, usually appear only as a splotch or speck in the sky and appear to move very slowly.

Although individual meteors can be seen on almost any night in an unpredictable fashion, meteor showers return every year at the same time. Their appearance is predictable because Earth passes through the same dust lanes again and again in its revolution around the Sun. These dust and debris lanes are where meteors originate.

The place in the sky where meteors appear to come from is known as the **radiant.** Constellations are used as markers to help viewers locate radiants. For example, the annual Leonid meteor shower is always located around the constellation Leo, the annual Perseid shower around the constellation Perseus, and so on. You'll need to know about radiants to locate the many meteor showers that can appear all over the sky. (See "Viewing Meteor Showers" on page 65.)

Although most meteors are no bigger than sand grains and pebbles, monstrously huge meteors occasionally bombard Earth. A meteorite (a meteor is officially called a meteorite if it survives

Unlucky Strikes

A whopping 3,306 tons (3,000 t) of meteoric material falls on Earth every day. But the odds of anybody being hit by a meteorite in any given year are about 10 trillion to 1. In 1860, a meteorite falling in Ohio killed a calf. In 1911, another falling in Egypt killed a dog. In Sylacauga, Alabama, on November 30, 1954, Mrs. E. Hulitt Hodges was taking a nap on her living-room couch when a 3-pound (1.3 kg) meteorite crashed through her roof, bounced off a radio, and struck her on the left thigh. She recovered enough to smile for newspaper photographs with her husband and the meteorite soon after. In 1992, the "Peekskill Fireball" crashed into a parked car in Peekskill, New York. The event was caught on videotape by several observers. No one was injured in the crash.

Viewing Meteor Showers

Meteor showers are always best seen when there is little or no Moon. And more can be seen after midnight than before.

The best way to view meteors is not with a telescope or binoculars but with the naked eye. Lie on your back on the ground or on a lounge chair and enjoy.

Lyrids

When: April 15–28

Where: Their origination point, or radiant, is in the northeast sky near the constellation Lyra. They are best seen late at night, after midnight. These are extremely bright meteors (they can be as bright as the planet Venus) and last a long time before flaring out. Many reach the ground as meteorites.

Eta Aquarids

When: May 6–11

Where: These flaring dust specks, also know as Halley's Dust, are remnants of Comet Halley. They were first recorded by the Chinese in A.D. 401. Meteors can be seen coming from the constellation Aquarius. This annual shower, one of the best of spring, is best viewed at midnight and after.

Perseids

When: August 8–15

Where: The Perseids meteor shower is one of the most popular showers, due not only to the warm evenings but the show itself. You can expect to see about 50 to 100 meteors per hour, with the highest numbers coming in the hours before dawn. The debris originates from the Comet Swift-Tuttle. Look in the northeast within the constellation Perseus.

Kappa Cygnids

When: August 20

Where: These brilliant yellow fireballs, which have been known to leave smoke trails lasting for several minutes, appear almost directly over-head at midnight. The average is 6 meteors per hour originating in the constellation Cygnus. Activity peaks around August 17–20.

Orionids

When: October 21–22

Where: This is another shower originating with Halley's comet. Watch for 20 to 25 meteors an hour from an area around the club of the constellation Orion.

Leonids

When: November 17–18

Where: This shower is made up of debris from the comet 55P/Temple-Tuttle. It becomes a meteor "storm" roughly every 33 years (and sometimes for a year or two following). In a storm, at least 1,000 meteors blaze across the sky per hour. In 1966, up to 40 meteors per second were seen for an hour. In 1999, part of the world saw a storm, while the United States (seeing it later) saw only a moderate shower. In 2001, 1,000 to 2,500 meteors per hour were seen, with a few exploding into dazzling **fire-balls** (fiery meteors), also called **bolides.** Viewers from around the world, including those in the United States, called it "breathtaking" and "spectacular." The radiant is around the constellation Leo.

Geminids

When: December 13–14

Where: If you can brave the cold, this is an excellent shower, with a peak of 60 to 80 meteors per hour. It's unusual because the meteors are debris from an asteroid instead of a comet. The radiant is in the constellation Gemini.

passage through Earth's atmosphere and lands on the ground) found in Willamette, Oregon, weighs about 15 tons (13.6 t). A meteorite found in Armanty, Outer Mongolia, weighs 20 tons (18 t). The Cape York Meteorite, found in Greenland by the explorer Robert Peary, weighs about 30 tons (27 t). The heaviest meteorite, called the Hoba Meteorite, found in Grootfontein, Namibia, weighs more than 50 tons (45 t).

Out-of-This-World Measurements

Distances to celestial objects are so vast that astronomers must abandon miles and kilometers and use their own units of measurement. Here are a few to ponder:

astronomical unit (AU) the distance between the Sun and Earth, or 93 million miles (150 million km). How many astronomical units are required to span the space between the Sun and Pluto at its most distant orbital position, 4.6 billion miles (7.4 billion km)?

light-year the distance traveled by a beam of light in one year: 5.9 trillion miles (9.5 trillion km). The most distant object we can see with the naked eye is the Andromeda Galaxy, located about 2.2 million light-years away.

parsec 3.26 light-years. *Parsec* stands for "parallax second," and explaining it involves some complex ideas. For now just remember it's a *very* long way.

MAKE A MOBILE OF THE SOLAR SYSTEM

Use crayons and paper to make a colorful model of the solar system.

WHAT YOU NEED   construction paper or heavy card stock

crayons, markers, or paint

scissors

needle

thread

cardboard or heavy card stock

adult helper

1 Use construction paper or heavy card stock paper to draw the nine planets and the Sun. You can't make a very good mobile using a truly accurate scale model, so instead draw each planet according to a rough scale. That is, the Sun should be the biggest, with Jupiter the next biggest and Saturn the next. Pluto would be the smallest.

2 Use crayons, markers, or paint to color each planet. Then cut the planets out.

3 Ask an adult to poke tiny holes in their tops with a needle.

4 Tie on lengths of thread. Connect the threads to two extra-long pieces of cardboard or heavy card stock and hang the planets and Sun in their correct order.

5 For added realism, you could add an asteroid belt between Jupiter and Mars and a comet ring, as described in the sections on the Kuiper Belt and the Oort Cloud, around the outer edge of the solar system.

6 Hang the entire construction from your ceiling or doorway.

Finding the Zodiacal Light

Anytime during the second half of August, set your alarm clock to go off from one to two hours before sunrise. Go outside and look toward the eastern horizon. If there is no moon and the sky where you live is especially dark (no city lights), you may be lucky enough to see the **zodiacal** (zoh-DYE-uh-kuhl) **light.**

This hazy band of light (it's unrelated to the Milky Way) is produced by sunlight reflecting off comet and asteroid dust in our solar system. You can also sometimes see the zodiacal light in the western sky about one and a half hours after sunset in late winter and early spring.

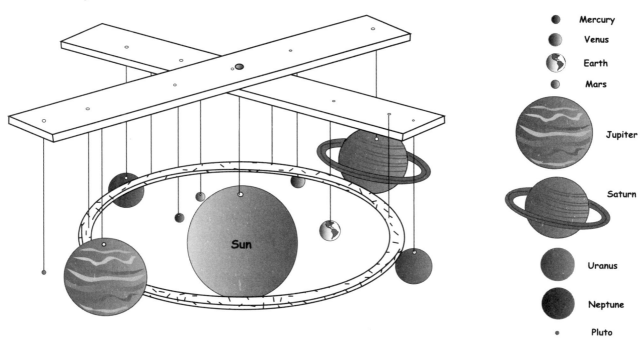

Mercury
Venus
Earth
Mars
Jupiter
Saturn
Uranus
Neptune
Pluto

Sun

Watching Satellites, the International Space Station, and the Shuttle Orbit Earth

Several hundred artificial satellites orbit Earth at any one time, relaying radio signals, monitoring the weather, collecting defense data, and so on. Because their surfaces reflect sunlight (they're high enough in the sky to be illuminated even though it's dark on the ground), the largest can easily be seen from most locations on Earth.

Many observers have as much fun watching orbiting satellites as meteors. Some satellites can create a flash as bright as or brighter than a meteor's, and their locations in the night sky are always predictable.

Among the best satellites to view are the International Space Station, the Space Shuttle, the Hubble Space Telescope, and iridium communications satellites, whose antennas flash brilliantly as they pass overhead. Check out the web site of heavens-above.com for places and times to look for passing satellites in your area. All you have to do is enter the name of your country and city in their program, and they'll give you all the viewing information you'll need to get started. Happy hunting!

Find Out More

Want to experience what it's like to train to be an astronaut? Check out U.S. Space Camp. This five-day program for kids offers simulated space shuttle missions, IMAX movies, rides in a one-sixth gravity chair, rocket building and launchings, experiments, and lectures on space. To attend any of the three camps (in Alabama, California, and Florida), you must be at least in the fourth grade or nine years old. (There are some programs available for younger children, but their parents must attend the camp with them.) For more information, check out spacecamp.com.

Part II

NEXT STOP: OUTER SPACE

As we say good-bye to our own backyard, the solar system and the surrounding Oort Cloud, all of the magnificent universe opens up before us. What is the universe? How far does it go? Does it end anywhere? And if so, what's on the other side?

One question haunts us above all others. It's a question philosophers and astronomers alike have wrestled with for centuries: Where did it all come from?

It started with a bang.

Scientists believe the universe began anywhere from 12 to 18 billion years ago when a pinpoint of matter expanded in a massive explosion called the **big bang.** The force of this incredible explosion can still be seen today. Just like debris thrown off in a bomb detonation, galaxies are hurtling away to ever deeper parts of the universe in all directions. And the galaxies farthest away are moving the fastest.

Nobody knows if this movement will ever stop. Some scientists say it will go on forever. Others say stars and galaxies will eventually stop and reverse direction. That is, one day they will all crash together and collapse back into one another, possibly leading to another big bang, which would start the process all over again.

That raises yet another question: Why?

What do you think?

4 Stars

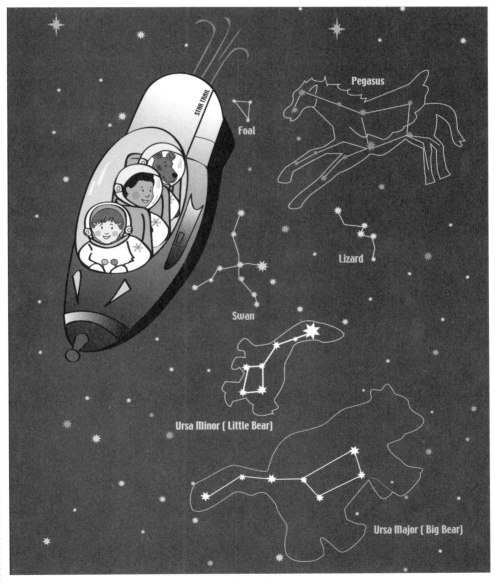

I n the next five minutes, 38,000 suns in the universe will die out forever. But these stars will be replaced by new stars, which are constantly being created.

As we learned earlier, stars are not mere twinkling lights in the sky, but suns just like our own. They appear small only because they are so very far away. The nearest star to Earth, other than our own Sun, is Proxima Centauri (which is visible only from the southern hemisphere of Earth). Traveling at the speed of light, it would take four years to reach it.

Some stars in the universe are much, much farther away from Earth. Even traveling at the speed of light, it would take not thousands, not millions, but billions of years to reach the most distant stars out there. Luckily for us, our spaceship can travel much faster than light.

Star Light, Star Bright, Which Kind of Star Do I See Tonight?

Astronomers classify stars in many different ways: by brightness, color, size, age, and so on.

Blue stars are the youngest stars, and they burn the hottest. Yellow stars, including our Sun, are middle aged and burn at a medium heat.

Red giant stars, such as Betelgeuse, are the largest and oldest stars and are in the process of dying. These are cooler than blue or yellow stars.

Many other types of stars populate the heavens. **White dwarfs,** for example, are small stars that have evolved beyond their red giant stage and have begun a long cooling and dying stage. These stars are collapsing into themselves to such a degree that a mere spoonful of matter from their cores would weigh as much as a small truck.

But not all dying stars become white dwarfs. Some particularly massive stars end their red giant stage with a gargantuan explosion called a **supernova** and become either neutron stars or black holes. (See the next section for a description of black holes.) A **neu-**tron star is a star that has collapsed into itself until it is only about 12 miles (19 km) in diameter. Yet its mass remains extremely dense, roughly equal that of our Sun. Neutron stars spin extremely fast, up to 30 times per second.

Neutron stars act as giant magnets and emit radiation and radio signals called "pulses." When these pulses can be detected from Earth, the neutron star is called a **pulsar.** Our galaxy contains an estimated 100,000 pulsars.

Because their signals are so regular and reliable, pulsars may one day be used as beacons to help keep interstellar spaceships on course.

A **variable star** is one that varies in brightness. Red giants are variable stars that expand and shrink over the course of a roughly two-year cycle. Betelgeuse in the constellation Orion is a variable red giant.

A **cepheid variable** is a yellow supergiant that expands and shrinks very quickly, every 3 to 50 days.

A **binary star** is actually two stars that revolve around each other.

When you look through a telescope at the galaxies that contain these stars, you are actually seeing them as they appeared from thousands to millions of years ago, not as they are now. That's because it takes that long for their light to reach Earth.

Some of the stars we see in the sky, in fact, may no longer even exist. The light an object gives off continues to travel through space, regardless of whether the object is still there or not.

Incredible as it sounds, if a star 100 light-years away exploded at this moment, we would not see it happen for a hundred years.

"Colored" Stars

Most people seem to think that the stars look all the same color from Earth. Not true. Under a dark sky (moonless, no city lights), if you look closely at each star and try to discern its color, you may be surprised to find that some appear red, some slightly golden, and some slightly blue. Rigel and Vega, for example, are very noticeably blue. Betelgeuse and Antares are at least golden orange, if not red. If your sky is clear and undistorted by heat or light clouds, you should be able to see dozens of stars with at least some color variations. Color sensitivity fades with age, so children may actually see more color than adults.

FIND THE SCORPION'S BEATING HEART

There's a scorpion threatening low in the sky. Spot it and its beating heart and you'll be close to some of the most astonishing sights in all the night sky, including the breathtaking center of our galaxy.

WHAT YOU NEED   your naked eye

WHAT TO LOOK FOR   The constellation Scorpius, the Scorpion, can be seen very low on the southern horizon in June, July, and August, from after 9:00 P.M. to around 11:00 P.M. or so.

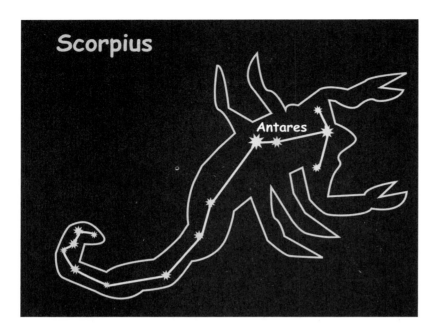

WHEN AND WHERE TO LOOK   Because this constellation hangs so low in the summer sky, it is difficult, but not impossible, to see in states north of New York. In northern areas, you'll need to find an unobstructed horizon. If you can find a high hill or mountaintop, all the better. Facing south, look for a group of stars shaped like a fishhook.

The "heart" of the Scorpion is unmistakable; it's a bloodred star called Antares (an-TARE-eez), which means "rival of Mars." Antares is a red supergiant, 700 times larger than our Sun. Quite appropriately, this star actually grows and contracts, or "pulsates." Thus you can see why astronomers like to call it the heart of the Scorpion.

See "Find What's in the Teapot" in the next chapter for the second and most exciting part of this star search.

Star Magnitude

A celestial object's brightness is called its **magnitude.** A magnitude number is assigned to all stars and planets. The higher the number, the dimmer the object. The lower the number, the brighter the object. The brightest objects of all actually have negative numbers. Thus Venus, the brightest object (other than the Moon) in the night sky, is assigned a magnitude of –3, and Jupiter, a –2. Stars with a magnitude of 4 are the faintest objects we can see with the naked eye near city lights. In dark, rural areas, we can make out 6th-magnitude stars. A powerful pair of binoculars will resolve 9th-magnitude stars. A 200-inch (508-cm) telescope can resolve 23rd-magnitude stars.

What are the five brightest stars in the sky?

The planets Venus, Mars, Jupiter, and Saturn are often the brightest sights in the sky. But among stars, the brightest are:

	Distance from Earth in Light-Years	Magnitude
Sirius	8.7	−1.5
Canopus	230.0	−0.7
Alpha Centauri	4.3	−0.3
Arcturus	38.0	0.06
Vega	27.0	0.04

Siriusly Bright

The brightest of all nighttime stars is located near the foot of the constellation Orion. It's called Sirius.

In Arabic, *sirius* means "scorching." Known as the Dog Star, Sirius has a magnitude of −1.50 and, at a distance of just 8.7 light-years, is the closest star visible to us in northern latitudes. (The Alpha Centauri system is actually closer but can only be seen from countries south of Earth's equator, such as Australia.) The ancient Greeks believed that Sirius helped the Sun to warm Earth in summer.

Even though Sirius is one of the closest stars to Earth, it is still out of reach of our fastest spacecraft. In fact, a ship traveling at 50,000 miles (80,500 km) per hour would take more than 100,000 years to reach this brilliant star.

Constellations

If you peer up at the night sky from Earth, stars grouped together sometimes appear to take on the shape of animals, objects, or mythological beings. Through the ages, people have seen backward question marks, upside-down Ws, club-wielding giants, big and little dippers. What exactly are all these figures, and do they mean anything?

These groups are called **constellations** (kahn-stuh-LAY-shuns). Constellations are kind of like connect-the-dot pictures. But the way the stars appear to group together is only a coincidence. Usually the stars in a group are completely unrelated to one another, and they may even be millions of light-years apart.

Still, constellations can be tremendously useful in helping us to locate various sights in the sky. Astronomers often use them as celestial road signs and landmarks.

The most famous constellation is probably Ursa Major. However, only part of Ursa Major is well known to most people. That part is commonly called the Big Dipper.

FIND THE BIG DIPPER

In the northern hemisphere, the Big Dipper is almost always visible in the sky, no matter what the season.

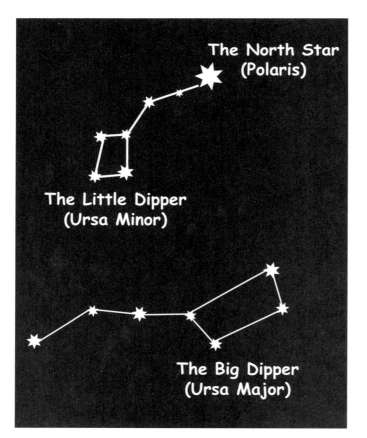

WHAT YOU NEED   your naked eye

In northern skies, facing north, you'll find the Big Dipper, or Ursa Major (which means the "Great Bear"), located almost overhead in an upside-down position. It looks like a small saucepan. The Big Dipper moves in circles. Here's where to spot it, according to the season:

Spring: high in the northeast

Summer: high in the northwest

Fall: lower in the northwest

Winter: very low in the northeast

FIND THE NORTH STAR

One of the most useful stars to know in the night sky is Polaris (poh-LAIR-us). Also known as the North Star or the Pole Star, it is 3,000 times bigger than our Sun and is located 680 light-years from Earth. All of the northern constellations appear to rotate around Polaris every 24 hours.

WHAT YOU NEED   your naked eye

The most famous thing about Polaris is that it's used as an orientation (location-finding) point. People use this 2nd-magnitude star to help point them in the direction of north and orient them to their position on the ground. You can find Polaris by first locating the Little Dipper. It's the last star in the Little Dipper's handle. If you have trouble locating the Little Dipper, just find the Big Dipper and follow the slant of the front of its "pan" almost three fist-widths to Polaris.

Who named the constellations, comets, and asteroids?

Most of the constellations of the northern hemisphere were visualized by the Sumerians and the Babylonians over 4,000 years ago. Most star names are of Arabic origin. In fact, an astronomer named al-Sufi, from the tenth century, is responsible for naming many of them. The Greeks and Romans named some, too.

The names of the stars and constellations of the southern hemisphere, on the other hand, were largely made up by European sailors. A Dutch mariner known as Pieter Dirkszoon Keyser mapped and named 12 southern constellations after his voyage to the East Indies in 1595.

Comets and asteroids are usually named after the people who discover them. It is very possible that you could spot a new asteroid and have it named after you. Backyard astronomers all over the world compete with one another for just this kind of honor.

FIND ONE OF THE MOST BEAUTIFUL SIGHTS IN THE SKY

*Most amateur astronomers agree: one of the most beautiful sights in all the night sky is a tight cluster of blue, jewel-like stars known as the Pleiades (PLEE-uh-deez). Located some 375 light-years from Earth, they are also known as the Seven Sisters, after the daughters of Atlas in Greek mythology. Atlas was the unfortunate soul who had to carry the heavens on his shoulders. His daughters, who were being pursued by the hunter Orion, were changed into doves, then lifted into the sky by Zeus and transformed into the famous star cluster. (A **cluster** is a group of stars sometimes numbering in the thousands.)*

WHAT YOU NEED   your naked eye

WHAT TO LOOK FOR If the sky is exceptionally clear, dark, and Moonless, you should be able to make out a cluster of six to nine stars (fewer if you're anywhere near city lights), although at first the Pleiades may be overlooked simply as a glowing "patch" frequently mistaken for the much smaller Little Dipper. Those with sharp vision may be able to make out 10 or more of the Pleiades. (Most people can spot only nine with the naked eye, but binoculars will reveal many more.)

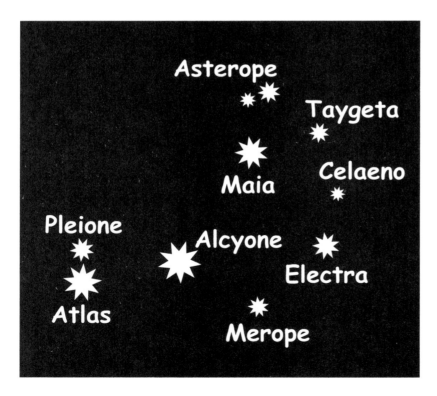

WHEN AND WHERE TO LOOK The Pleiades can be seen about halfway up in the sky, to the right and above Orion (see "Find the Marvels of Orion" in the next chapter) and just above a V-formation of stars. Peer toward the east early in the season: in September after 11:00 P.M., in October after 9:00 P.M., and from November through March, moving increasingly toward the west as the season progresses, from nightfall on. (Also in August after 1:00 A.M.)

The brightest stars in the cluster are Alcyone, Asterope Atlas, Celaeno, Electra, Maia, Merope, Pleione, and Taygeta. Moonlight or city lights may drown out all but Alcyone, so viewing conditions must be near perfect to appreciate this sight.

The Pleiades provide a great test of your eyes. The more stars you can see in the cluster, the better your eyes' light-gathering power. As we age, the eyes take much longer to adjust to the dark and gather faint light. So don't be surprised when the youngest in your viewing group manages to make out the most stars.

FIND MORE STARS IN THE PLEIADES WITH BINOCULARS

Now that you've had a good look at the Pleiades with your naked eye, try finding more with binoculars.

WHAT YOU NEED   binoculars

Looking through the binoculars, you may be surprised to see that stars you thought were individuals are actually two or more stars. The sky holds many stars that can be visually split like this. All it takes is a sharper focus. See what other stars outside of the Pleiades you can split.

Black Holes

Black holes are the stuff astronomical legends are made of. They are weird. Really weird.

A **black hole** is not really a hole but a giant star that's burned up all of its fuel and then collapsed into itself. Simply put, it's a supertight, superdense ball of matter.

A black hole's gravity may be the most powerful force in the universe. It's so powerful it can literally tear nearby stars in two and suck the pieces into its core. It can not only bend light but prevent it from escaping altogether. That's what makes a black hole look virtually invisible.

Telescopes and Spectroscopes

Astronomers use many different kinds of instruments to view the universe. **Optical telescopes** use lenses and mirrors to magnify dim light and bring distant celestial objects into focus. The twin Keck Telescopes on the summit of Mauna Kea in Hawaii, among the most powerful in the world, have the ability to see the headlights of a car parked 15,000 miles (24,000 km) away. The Hubble Space Telescope, which orbits Earth, is also an optical telescope. Because it's located well above Earth's distorting atmosphere, it has brought us the clearest pictures of space yet.

Radio telescopes, in contrast, are more like antennas and have no lenses or mirrors. Instead, these giant, dish-shaped structures gather and magnify radio (or electromagnetic) waves from galaxies, stars, black holes, and other objects, which are then analyzed with a computer. The biggest dish radio telescope in the world is the Arecibo Telescope in Puerto Rico. It measures about 1,000 feet (304 m) in diameter.

Radio telescopes, like optical telescopes, can be joined together to increase their power. Such multiple units, whether optical or radio, are called **interferometers.** The VLA, or Very Large Array, is an interferometer comprising 27 radio telescopes aligned to work together on railroad tracks in southern New Mexico.

Unlike optical or radio telescopes, **spectroscopes** are instruments astronomers use to separate light into its component colors, creating a rainbow or spectrum. They are used, among other things, to reveal what elements a celestial body is made of. Different elements, such as hydrogen or deuterium, emit or absorb light at different wavelengths. Because each element is unique, it leaves its own unique "signature" in a star's light, which scientists can analyze and identify. A spectroscope attached to one of the Keck Telescopes can distinguish 30,000 different colors.

Spectroscopes are also used to study the motion of galaxies. When a galaxy moves away from Earth, its light has a longer wavelength than a stationary one, while galaxies moving toward Earth have shorter wavelengths.

Can you imagine a power so strong that it could actually keep a light beam from leaving its grip? Now imagine gravity so immensely strong that it could actually stop time. Scientists think this may happen in a black hole.

Because a black hole could stretch our spaceship like taffy and then suck us into its core, we'll stay several million miles away to stay safe!

While young black holes may be composed of a single collapsed star, older ones may be made from hundreds or even thousands. Those nestled at the centers of galaxies have gulped down millions of nearby stars. These are super eating machines with gargantuan appetites.

Although black holes can't be seen directly, scientists can guess their existence by monitoring the havoc that goes on around them, including storms of roiling gas, billion-degree temperatures, fast-moving and exploding stars, and superpowerful radio signals. These all point to something truly cataclysmic nearby.

Collapsed Suns and Black Holes

In the 1930s, Grote Reber, a ham radio operator living in Wheaton, Illinois, erected the first true radio telescope—in his mother's backyard.

Reber had been intrigued by the findings of a radio engineer named Karl Jansky (1905–1950). While working on a project for transatlantic radio telephone service in 1932, Jansky picked up strange signals through a large antenna he had built. The mysterious signals seemed to come from the Milky Way, especially from its center.

Reber mapped Jansky's and other radio emissions from around the cosmos. Like Jansky, he found the strongest signals coming from the core of our galaxy. Another powerful source was in the constellation Cygnus.

What could make such strong signals? Reber didn't know. Nor did anyone else at the time. But his and Jansky's work marked the beginning of the new science of **radio astronomy,** the study of electromagnetic radiation from space.

Now, after decades of study, scientists think they've figured out where the most powerful signals are coming from: black holes.

Most galaxies are thought to contain black holes at their centers. Our own galaxy contains a whopper. Scientists calculate that its mass must equal 2 or even 3 billion of our Suns. That's not a misprint. That means 3 billion Suns all squished together in one supertight blob.

FIND THE BLACK HOLE IN OUR GALAXY

Of course you can't see a black hole, but you can see where this monster is located.

WHAT YOU NEED   binoculars

WHAT TO LOOK FOR   Use the binoculars to find the star group known as the Teapot (in the constellation Sagittarius, see "What's in the Teapot" in the next chapter for a description of how to find this constellation).

WHEN AND WHERE TO LOOK   Look near the southern horizon in summer. Just to the right of the star that marks the point in the Teapot's spout is the center of our galaxy—and what may be one of nature's all-time weirdest creations.

Brown Dwarfs

They wander throughout space, sometimes alone, sometimes near a star. Most are larger than the largest planets. Trillions are believed to populate the universe. Indeed, they're so common they're thought to at least equal the number of stars.

Yet nobody has ever actually seen one with the naked eye. In fact, the first wasn't even discovered until 1995.

What are they? Why, brown dwarfs, of course.

Strange name. Strange worlds.

A **brown dwarf** is neither a star nor a planet, but a gaseous body classified in between. Many scientists call these mysterious spheres "failed stars." That's because they have almost enough mass to flare into permanent suns. But not quite.

Unlike stars, brown dwarfs give off only a dim, reddish light. This feeble light is sometimes drowned out if there is another, brighter star nearby. So brown dwarfs are tough to see from Earth.

To find a brown dwarf, astronomers must mask any nearby star's glare with a device called a coronagraph. Sometimes they can only guess that a brown dwarf exists, not by eye, but by the erratic motion of another, visible star.

Find Out More

Some of the most eye-popping sights in space have been captured by the Hubble Space Telescope. Launched by the space shuttle, this massive telescope orbits in space 380 miles (608 km) above Earth, well above our light-obscuring atmosphere. It was this remote-controlled marvel of technology that discovered the first black hole and the first planet outside of our solar system. Find out more about Hubble's discoveries and see great views of lots of other celestial objects at Hubble's web site: www.stsci.edu/gallery.

Five of these Jupiter-sized or larger objects can be found in the area of the Big Dipper and in the constellations Leo, Virgo, and Corvus. Twenty-two of these strange worlds have been located in the Pleiades star cluster. At least 100 billion more are thought to exist in the Milky Way Galaxy alone.

It's time to move deeper into space. Close you eyes and turn on your imagination. We've got a long way to travel.

Earth's Mysterious Second "Sun"?

One exciting but troubling possibility: even though we cannot see it, a brown dwarf may be lurking closer to Earth than the closest star, Proxima Centauri. Scientists think it's a strong possibility because it turns out that most stars have companions, or twins. So where is ours?

The troubling part is, if such a nearby brown dwarf exists, it may turn out to be the force that has been knocking comets out of their orbits in the Oort Cloud and sending them crashing to Earth every few million years. This idea or hypothesis is known as the Nemesis Hypothesis. And the brown dwarf that may be hiding nearby? It's nicknamed the "Death Star."

Does the Death Star really exist? Only time and lots more searching will tell.

Galaxies, Quasars, and Nebulae

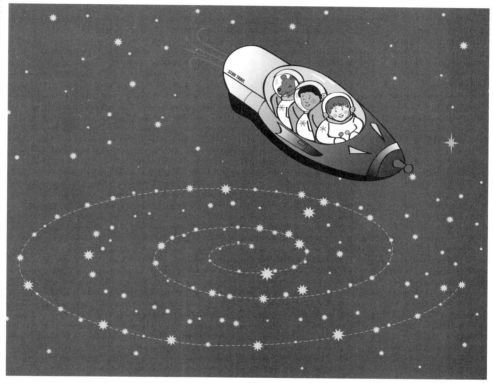

As we fly in our spaceship, stars appear in the distance, often in groups. Stars massed together in large conglomerations are called open clusters or globular clusters. Open clusters may contain up to a thousand stars. Globular clusters may contain as many as a million.

Stars massed together in groups of millions, billions, or even trillions, on the other hand, are known as **galaxies.** Galaxies have been called "island universes." Seen through a powerful telescope, galaxies often look like giant whirlpools or globes of light.

We live in a giant spiral-shaped galaxy called the Milky Way. More than 400 billion stars in addition to our Sun reside here.

Before the twentieth century, people believed the Milky Way was the whole universe. When astronomers later discovered not thousands or millions but billions of other galaxies, each containing billions or even trillions of individual suns, people were thunderstruck. Space was a much bigger place than anyone ever dreamed.

The Greeks called the portion of our galaxy that they could see in the sky the Milky Way because it resembles a spray of milk or *gala*. *Gala* is where we get the word *galaxy*.

Our solar system is located about halfway out (roughly 26,000 light-years) from the center of the galaxy on one of the Milky Way's spiral arms. You can see a part of this spiral arm on any dark night in summer if you are away from city lights. It looks like a hazy or, indeed, "milky" river of light stretching from horizon to horizon.

This dim trail is actually the light from millions of stars. The individual stars are difficult to see because they are so far away. Peer through a good pair of binoculars or a telescope, however, and many of these stars will appear.

From deep in outer space, our galaxy looks like a whirlpool with a hazy bar across its middle. Many galaxies in the universe, in fact, look like this. These types of galaxies are called barred spirals.

Galaxy Types

Galaxies are classified into seven types. Spiral galaxies are shaped like whirlpools, with loose or tight spiral arms and small or large centers. Barred spirals have arms that swirl out from the ends of straight bars running through their centers. The Milky Way is thought to be a barred spiral. Lenticular galaxies are disk shaped like spirals, but don't have the actual spiral arms. Elliptical galaxies have no apparent spirals either but instead of being flat like lenticular galaxies, they are shaped like blobs or eggs. Giant ellipticals are the most massive galaxies and have many more stars than spiral galaxies. Irregular galaxies have no specific shape and may look like vague clouds. Peculiar galaxies have weird or sometimes inexplicable shapes. The Cartwheel Galaxy, for example, looks very much like a wagon wheel. Its shape was caused by a second galaxy passing through its center. Seyfert galaxies are spirals with small but unusually brilliant nuclei (centers). Their cores are extremely active, with gas and dust moving at speeds of 6,000 miles (9,656 km) per second. These galaxies produce enormous energy and emit powerful radio emissions.

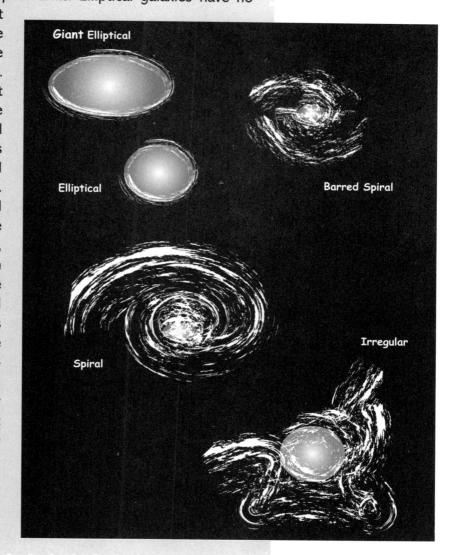

Giant Elliptical

Elliptical

Barred Spiral

Spiral

Irregular

FIND WHAT'S IN THE BOWL OF THE BIG DIPPER

Next time you're out after dark on a clear night, peer up at the Big Dipper and get ready for a surprise.

WHAT YOU NEED   binoculars

Although you can't see them with the naked eye, at least a million galaxies can be found in the area of the Big Dipper's bowl alone. You can see M51, or the Whirlpool Galaxy, with binoculars, just underneath the very end of the Big Dipper's handle.

COVER UP A TRILLION STARS WITH A SINGLE PENNY

Located 2.9 million light-years from Earth, the Andromeda Galaxy contains a breathtaking number of stars.

WHAT YOU NEED   binoculars or telescope
penny

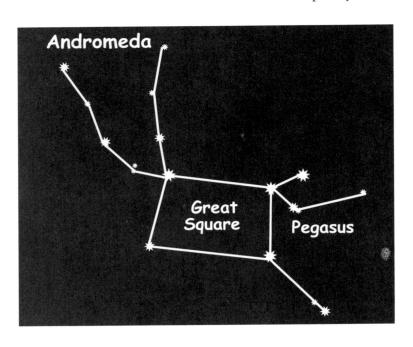

At first glance with the naked eye, the Andromeda Galaxy appears as a single hazy star. Upon closer inspection with binoculars or a telescope, you'll see that it is something quite different.

If you hold a penny at arm's length to cover this hazy patch, you have obscured from your vision at least 400 billion and possibly as many as 1 trillion stars.

Although this spiral galaxy remains fuzzy even with binoculars, many amateur astronomers report having the hairs on the back of their necks stand up whenever they look at it—not only because of the breathtaking number of stars it contains, but because the light from those stars traveled more than 2 million light-years to reach their eyes. As mind-boggling as it sounds, when you look at the Andromeda Galaxy, you're looking at something not as it appears now, but as it appeared over 2 million years ago.

WHAT TO LOOK FOR   You can spot the constellation Andromeda by first locating a constellation in the shape of a big **W**, known as Cassiopeia. Just below the big **W** is a **V**-shaped constellation, Andromeda. To the west of the **V** shape is M31, the Andromeda Galaxy, visible with the naked eye as a fuzzy white patch. It is the most distant celestial object you can see from Earth without a telescope.

WHEN AND WHERE TO LOOK   In July and August, from nightfall on in the east (after 11:00 P.M. in the east in June), then progressing toward nearly overhead from nightfall in the fall to an overhead westerly position in winter.

Quasars

Traveling out beyond the local stars of our own galaxy, and then beyond the Andromeda Galaxy, and then beyond the billions of other galaxies beyond Andromeda, we peer out our ship's windows and begin to see not nothingness, but some of the brightest and most mysterious objects in the universe.

The most distant objects astronomers can see in space are **quasars,** located several billion light-years from Earth. The word *quasar* is derived from the term "quasi-stellar object," but these objects aren't stars. In fact, scientists are still trying to figure out just what they are.

The brightest quasar known is one found in the constellation Virgo. The light it gives off is equivalent to that of 1.5 quadrillion suns.

What's beyond quasars? Nobody knows yet. But astronomers are looking.

Nebulae

A **nebula** is a great gas-and-dust cloud in space. A nebula can be either a remnant of exploded stars, such as the Crab Nebula, or a kind of nursery where newborn stars are formed, such as the Orion Nebula. Some nebulae are so massive that they defy imagination. Take the Horsehead Nebula, for example. A billion of our solar systems could fit inside of it.

Be prepared, our next journey will take us on the most exciting search of all: the search for life.

FIND THE MARVELS OF ORION

"Fee, fi, fo, fum, I smell the blood of an Englishman!" You may be reminded of that line the first time you lay eyes on Orion, the Hunter.

WHAT YOU NEED   star chart
                      binoculars

WHAT TO LOOK FOR   Dominating the winter heavens, this barrel-chested giant appears to be wielding a club high in his right hand and holding a lion's pelt or a shield in his left. Orion in Greek mythology was a giant and the son of the sea god Poseidon.

After the Big Dipper, Orion is probably the best known of all the constellations. And it's not only a snap to locate, it also holds a wealth of truly awe-inspiring objects.

WHEN AND WHERE TO LOOK   In the northern hemisphere, Orion can be seen at a reasonable hour (9:00 P.M. or earlier) from November to April. For the rest of the year, you'll have to stay up much later. (Well past the bedtime of kids and many adults. Still, if you and your parents are up to the task, consult a star chart for viewing times during warmer months.) Face south and peer about halfway up the sky. First, look for three bright stars grouped closely together in a diagonal line. This is Orion's Belt.

The stars of the belt are (starting from the giant's right, your left) Alnitak (al-NYE-tack), Alnilam (al-NILE-am), and Mintaka

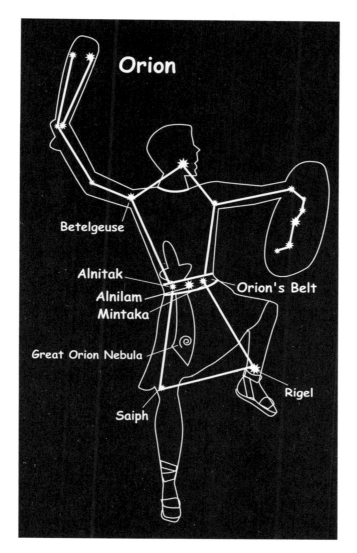

(MIN-tack-uh). Translated from Arabic, these names mean "the belt," or "the belt of pearls."

Below the belt are the giant's feet (some call them his knees), a second-magnitude star called Saiph (safe), and a very bright bluish, first-magnitude star called Rigel (RYE-jell).

Rigel is not only one of the hottest of all stars, but it shines with an intensity 150,000 times that of our Sun. If placed next to our Sun, Rigel would appear 50 times larger. It would, quite literally, roast Earth. Lucky for us, Rigel is a comfortably distant 1,300 light-years away.

Above the belt, at Orion's shoulder, is a cooler although much larger star than Rigel. This distinctly red star is called Betelgeuse (beetle juice), otherwise known as the armpit of the giant. (Can you guess why the ancients called it that?)

Betelgeuse is an old red supergiant star fast approaching its retirement years. Huge jets of matter are believed to be blowing off the star and into space, a clear sign of aging. But such loss of mass (the equivalent of an Earth-sized chunk every three years) has done little to diminish the awesome dimensions of Betelgeuse; its diameter is more than 300 million miles (482,803,200 km).

Betelgeuse is one of a class of stars known as variables. That means that its brightness changes over time, becoming brighter and dimmer over regular intervals.

Betelgeuse is actually contracting and expanding as it struggles to strike a balance between the powerful gravity forces sucking it in and the massive nuclear forces blowing it out. Sometimes Betelgeuse swells to twice its normal size (imagine if our own Sun did that). Astronomers can detect such bloating by noting a change in the star's magnitude, or brightness. However, the variation in Betelgeuse is usually very small and difficult to detect without careful observation.

If your skies are free of moonlight, haze, or city lights, you should be able to see the dimmer stars that mark Orion's uplifted right arm and club, the shield or lion's pelt in his left hand, and the sword hanging from his belt. If you can't see these stars, use binoculars.

Once you've identified the complete picture of Orion (some say Orion looks more like a rampaging robot than a man), take a close look at the central star in his sword. It should appear misty.

That star is really not a star at all, but a giant cloud called the Great Orion Nebula. This gargantuan mass of gas and dust—some 20,000 times larger than our entire solar system—is thought to be a nursery for newborn stars. The nebula's eerie green swirls and wreaths are clearly visible through powerful binoculars.

Of the many stars hiding within the nebula's cloak, only Theta is readily seen through low-powered lenses. Theta is actually made up of four stars, forming the configuration of a trapezoid. Astronomers call this mini-constellation the Trapezium.

Another great gas cloud in Orion deserves special mention even though it's invisible to the naked eye. Located around the star known as Alnitak in Orion's Belt is the world-famous Horsehead Nebula.

As you might guess, the cloud is named for its distinctive shape—like a giant horse's head. This head is so huge that a billion of our solar systems could fit inside of it.

Unfortunately, the only way to see the Horsehead is through a large telescope using long-exposure photography. But to many stargazers, just knowing where this great galactic stallion is corralled provides a special thrill in itself.

FIND WHAT'S IN THE TEAPOT

Just east of Antares, which we described in the activity "Find the Scorpion's Beating Heart" in the previous chapter, is the constellation Sagittarius. There may be no more awe-inspiring place in all the night sky through which to sweep a telescope or pair of binoculars. It holds riches beyond imagination.

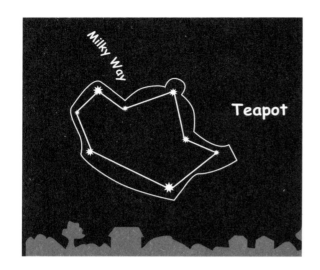

WHAT YOU NEED   binoculars

WHAT TO LOOK FOR   To find the Teapot, a star group within Sagittarius, just look for what appears to be a giant teapot pouring its contents down on Earth.

WHEN AND WHERE TO LOOK   Very low in the southern sky from after 9:00 P.M. to midnight from June to August, and from 9:00 to about 11:00 P.M. in September.

As you look at the sky in the area of Sagittarius (as well as Scorpius), you'll notice a hazy band of light. What you're seeing is one of the spiral arms of our own galaxy, the Milky Way. Gaze near the Teapot's spout and you peer toward the center, or nucleus, of our galaxy. (The center itself is obscured by thick gas clouds.)

The area within and around the Teapot offers an extraordinarily rich field of sights. Here, with binoculars, you can see M8,

otherwise known as the Lagoon Nebula, a large starlit gas cloud just above the Teapot's lid. Directly above is M20, or the Trifid Nebula, which is another illuminated gas cloud, and M24, or the Small Sagittarius Star Cloud. Here you'll see the milky light from over a million stars.

Messier Objects

Charles Messier (1730–1817) was a comet hunter who, in 1758, peered through a telescope and noticed a cloudy patch of light in the constellation Taurus. Although it looked something like a comet, its fixed position proved it was something else. What was it?

Apparently Messier didn't much care. What he found was a nebula, one of many such space objects that held little fascination for him. To avoid confusing these objects with comets, he cataloged them all in his sky charts. Over the years, he and another astronomer cataloged 103 such objects, and since then, modern scientists have added seven more.

Today these "objects" are among astronomers' most sought-after sights in the sky. When you see them in a star chart, they're listed either by their name (the Andromeda Galaxy, for example) or by a number, preceded by *M* for Messier, as in M31. These galaxies, nebulae, and star clusters contain a wealth of information about the universe. One of the great challenges for amateur stargazers is to locate all of the Messier objects in a single night.

Messier discovered more than a dozen comets. But these are all but forgotten. Known by every astronomer today, however, is the catalog illustrating the objects that made such a mess of Messier's sky, the very objects he worked so hard to ignore.

MAKE YOUR OWN SIGHT CATALOG

Start a sight catalog with drawings of Orion.

WHAT YOU NEED   flashlight covered with red cellophane

crayons or markers

drawing pad

1   Using the flashlight covered with red cellophane, draw all of the stars and sights of Orion as they appear in the sky on the pad. Label everything carefully for future reference. This will help you to remember them all, and later you can explain what you know to your friends.

2   Add to your catalog other interesting space sights, making your own hand-drawn star maps, diagrams, and drawings.

Test Your Space IQ

How much do you know about space? Take this quiz and then check your answers on page 98.

Questions

1. How many planets are found in our solar system?

2. How many of the planets can you name? Score 1 point for each. Score 5 bonus points if you can name all of the planets in order, from the closest to the Sun to the farthest away.

3. How far from Earth is the Hubble Space Telescope?

4. What's a galaxy?

5. What's a nebula?

6. Is there such a thing as a shooting star? If so, what is it?

7. What's an asteroid?

8. How does the Sun produce its heat and light?

9. What's a light-year?

10. The tides on Earth are caused mostly by what object?

11. What's a comet?

Do Something about Light Pollution

On a dark, clear night with no Moon, the average person should be able to see about 3,000 stars. Unfortunately, only those of us living in the country can experience such splendor. Why? City light pollution is literally "fading out" the night sky. Stars, planets, galaxies, and nebulae are virtually vanishing behind the ever-glowing glare. The result? Most city and suburb dwellers are lucky if they can see 100 stars. Some city dwellers may even see as few as five.

Don't let our view of the heavens disappear forever. Many lights left on at night are unnecessary. You can start by turning out any outdoor lights you don't need around your own home. Here are some other things you can do to help:

1. Write a report on light pollution for school and ask your classmates to talk to their parents about it.

2. Write letters to the editors of your local newspaper, complaining about city, corporate, and residential lights left on unnecessarily all night.

3. Write or call your local legislators to ask about passing new laws requiring that any new outdoor lights be shielded to the ground.

4. If an outdoor light must be kept on at night, have a parent point it down toward the ground or shield it. Light falling in a neighbor's yard is called "light trespass," and more and more people are objecting to it. In some places, it is even illegal. Lights with motion detectors, which only come on when a person or animal passes by them, are an alternative.

5. Start a neighborhood "Turn Off the Lights, See the Stars" night. If you live in a safe community, you may be able to organize your neighbors to take part in an annual "Shut Off All the Lights" night so everybody can ooh and aah at the stars from their front yards. Contact your city council and ask if it would be possible to have a few local street lights turned off for two hours during one evening in summer each year. It could be the start of a beautiful new tradition.

6. Join the International Dark Sky Association, a nonprofit organization working to regulate nighttime lighting. Write to them for other helpful ideas. E-mail: ida@darksky.org. Visit their web page at: wwwdarksky.org/ida/ida_2/index.html. Or write: 3225 N. First Avenue, Tucson, AZ 85719.

Find Out More

Check out what's up in the sky tonight, plus daily space news, star charts, photo galleries, astronomical equipment, and more at astronomy.com.

For space news, missions, launches, photo galleries, reference information, activities, games, entertainment, message boards, and more, visit space.com.

Want a flight suit like the astronauts wear? How about a helmet? Freeze-dried space food? (Even french fries.) You can buy these, plus patches, hats, toys, model kits, books, and more, at thespacestore.com.

Answers

1. Nine

2. (In order) Mercury, Venus, Earth, Mars, Jupiter, Saturn, Uranus, Neptune, Pluto. Sometimes Neptune and Pluto alternate as the most distant from the Sun.

3. 380 miles (612 km)

4. A conglomeration or large group of stars, sometimes numbering in the millions or even billions

5. A gas-and-dust cloud in space

6. There is no such thing as a shooting star. However, meteors are sometimes inaccurately called this.

7. A large chunk of rock drifting in space

8. Through the process of nuclear fusion

9. The distance a beam of light travels in one year

10. The Moon

11. A large chunk of ice, rock, and dust that orbits the Sun

Extrasolar Planets and the Search for Extraterrestrial Life

The first extrasolar planets (those outside of our solar system) were discovered revolving around a pulsar in the constellation Virgo by radio astronomers Alexander Wolszczan and Dale Frail in 1991. Scientists have since discovered more than 50 other planets orbiting various stars.

One of the newly discovered worlds, located 123 light-years from Earth (in the constellation Serpens), is a monstrous sphere with 17 times the mass of Jupiter. As big as it is, it should have been easy to find, right? Actually, it has never been seen. Nor have any of the other extrasolar planets.

We, as astronauts of the imagination, are the only explorers to lay eyes on them. How, then, do scientists back on Earth know they're there?

Unlike stars, planets give off only reflected light. With planets outside of our solar system, that reflected light is too dim to detect even with the most powerful telescopes.

Rather, astronomers must guess these planets' existence by their gravitational effects. Like brown dwarfs, planets exert "pull" on the stars they revolve around. When a distant star "wobbles" mysteriously, scientists know that something nearby is tugging at it—possibly a planet. (Scientists can detect these slight wobbles through spectroscopy.) Because this effect is so subtle, so far scientists have only been able to detect the very largest, Jupiter-size planets.

Sometimes scientists are able to detect when a star's light dims temporarily. Often when this happens, it means a large body—a planet, a brown dwarf, or another star—has passed in front of it. Locating new planets this way is called the transit method.

Astronomers are fond of saying that finding an extrasolar world is like "spotting a gnat on a searchlight a thousand miles away." It ain't easy.

Little is known about extrasolar planets now, but scientists are always devising new ways to learn more about distant celestial objects. Planet-searching devices in the future will float deep in space and will include supertelescopes comprising several lenses bound together.

With the discovery of these new planets outside our solar system, one thing is now certain: billions if not trillions of similar planets are likely to populate the universe.

Is there life on other worlds?

With so many potential worlds out there, some must surely hold life, right? Probably, say scientists.

Even from our distant vantage point, scientists are good at figuring out which planets may hold life and which could not.

Planets too close to their suns are likely to have all their water boiled away. Planets too far away would probably be frozen solid. Tiny planets are unable to hold on to their atmospheres. Large planets tend to develop thick poisonous atmospheres of hydrogen.

What scientists look for, then, is a "Goldilocks" or "just-right" planet. Earth is just such a planet.

A "habitable" planet should not only be of the right size and distance from its sun, it should also have a very large planet nearby to help block asteroids. In our own system, Jupiter has absorbed many large space rocks that otherwise might have crashed into Earth.

If such a habitable planet could be seen, its atmosphere could be read (even from as far away as Earth) by analyzing its light spectrum. Evidence of oxygen (produced by plants), along with carbon dioxide, water, and methane, would strongly indicate life. NASA scientists believe we will locate such planets within 15 years.

Search for Extraterrestrials

Is there intelligent life out there? As we cruise in our interstellar spaceship, one thing is striking. With so many trillions of suns—and, very likely, trillions of planets—the universe must be near teeming with intelligent life-forms. If not, as the famous astronomer Carl Sagan (1934–1996) was fond of saying, what an awful waste of space!

Scientists involved in the **SETI** (Search for Extraterrestrial Intelligence) program have been "listening" for alien signals from space for years. The signals, of course, are radio signals. To receive them, radio astronomers use huge dishlike antennas, just like those seen in the movie *Contact*. Astronomers have listened closely to signals from celestial bodies all over the heavens, but so far no alien-made signals have been captured.

Find Out More

To find out more about how real scientists are searching for aliens, check out these two web sites: the Planetary Society of Pasadena, California (http://seti.planetary.org) and the SETI Institute of Mountain View, California (www.seti-inst.edu).

Recently scientists have begun looking for signals from space. These scientists think really intelligent beings would flash signals in the form of laser beams. Such optical signals are easier to detect than radio signals. Giant antennas are unnecessary, and all that is needed is a small device attached to a regular telescope. So far, no luck. But these astronomers are keeping their eyes peeled.

SEARCH FOR EXTRATERRESTRIALS FROM YOUR HOME COMPUTER

Incredible as it sounds, you can help SETI scientists search for extra-terrestrial space signals through your own computer at home.

WHAT YOU NEED   free computer program downloaded from
http://setiathome.ssl.berkeley.edu/

Once you've downloaded the program, your computer's screen-saver device will begin processing signals from the giant radio telescope in Arecibo, Puerto Rico. You'll even be able to watch the signals being processed right on your screen. As of this writing, over 2 million home computer users have signed on to become armchair radio astronomers.

Was that a UFO?

What are the odds that that mysterious light you saw in the sky last night was a UFO, an unidentified flying object or spaceship from another planet?

UFOs are breathlessly reported to the authorities every day. Despite observers' confidence in what they have witnessed, 99 out of 100 sightings either turn out to be hoaxes or are easily explained. And the remaining 1 percent of sightings that go unexplained? Sometimes UFOs are so fleeting, they prove impossible for investigators to track. But just because this small number of sightings goes unexplained doesn't mean that they're spaceships from other worlds.

Investigators have accumulated a long list of artificial and natural phenomena that can fool people into thinking they've seen something that they haven't. Coupled with long distances, poor lighting, overworked imaginations, and wishful thinking, it's easy to convince ourselves that a "strange light" in the sky is a visitor from another planet.

Think carefully about the following list and check off all items you think are or have been mistaken for UFOs. Then guess the top two.

❑ The planet Venus

❑ Hordes of glowing moths

❑ Weather balloons

❑ Satellite debris reentering Earth's atmosphere and burning up

❑ Hot air balloons

❑ Blimps

❑ Lenticular clouds (lens-shaped clouds sometimes seen near mountains)

❑ Meteorites

❑ Flocks of geese

❑ Emergency flares

❑ Airplanes

❑ Satellites in orbit (visible during twilight hours)

❑ Kites

❑ Military test craft

❑ Swamp gas igniting due to atmospheric static electricity

❑ Ball lightning

❑ Noctilucent clouds (very high clouds that glow at night due to atmospheric conditions)

Answer: All of the above. The most common UFOs turn out simply to be airplanes or the planet Venus.

Scientists only recently discovered that moths traveling in large groups at night, in swarms 1 mile (1.6 km) or more in length, can sometimes be charged by static electricity and glow in the dark. They may, in fact, be responsible for a fairly large number of unexplained sightings. Any number of other "natural phenomena" may be responsible for UFO sightings. In time we may discover what they are.

Finally, keep in mind the mind-boggling distances between other solar systems and our own. Any space journey by aliens would likely take decades, centuries, or even millennia before reaching Earth. From what we now know about space travel, such a feat may be beyond the realm of what's physically possible.

CREATE YOUR OWN FAKE UFO

With just a few simple tools you can see how "hoaxers" take photographs of fake UFOs. You can even fool your friends. (But do tell them about your little tricks when you're done.)

WHAT YOU NEED: old hubcap from an abandoned automobile *or* 2 paper plates glued together and spray-painted a metallic silver

camera

fishing pole and line

tape

coins

window with panoramic view

flashlight

helper

1 Toss the hubcap or glued paper plates into the air (make sure the sky and a little bit of ground is in the background) and photograph your "UFO" in "midflight." Or use a fishing pole and line to suspend the UFO in midair as it is photographed. You may be surprised to see how invisible fishing line can be under the right lighting conditions.

2 Use your imagination and see if you can find other items around the house that might, in a photograph, pass for an alien spaceship. For example, another hoaxer's method is to simply tape pennies, dimes, or quarters (hide the tape on the back of the coins) to a car or house window and then photograph them against the sky and panoramic background, such as a city or mountain range. Make sure the window is sparkling clean and be sure not to include the window's frame in the shot. If you can, focus the camera's lens so the shot will be just slightly blurry. *Voilà!* UFOs in flight!

3 To stage an even simpler "UFO" shot, have a friend stand behind you and shine a flashlight beam onto a clean window that allows a view of the sky. Photograph the light on the window. *Presto!* A mysterious "light in the sky" that your friends will not be able to explain.

Greetings from Earth, the Voyager Spacecraft

The *Voyager 1* space probe was launched in 1977 to study the planets of our solar system. Traveling at 38,718 miles (62,310.5 km) per hour, it performed all of its intended duties long ago and now soars beyond the orbit of Pluto, more than 6.8 billion miles (10.9 billion km) away. It should continue flying into outer space indefinitely. *Voyager 2* was launched shortly afterward and is now more than 5.3 billion miles (8.5 billion km) from Earth and headed in the opposite direction from *Voyager 1*'s flight path.

Both spacecraft are now Earth's ambassadors. They carry special copper phonograph disks containing greetings from humans in 55 languages, and information about Earth. Among this information are animal and nature sounds, music, and more. It is hoped that intelligent aliens will one day find the space probes, decipher the instructions for "playing" the disks, and learn all about us, including who we are and where we're located.

How far will the Voyagers have traveled after a million years? Will they travel far enough to have a close brush with other planets? With other life-forms? With intelligent life-forms?

One thing is clear. Even after a million years—even after a billion years—their voyage will have taken them no farther than the inner harbor of a vast and possibly infinite ocean of space.

Assuming both spacecraft could survive indefinitely (not likely), they could cruise at their present speed for hundreds of billions of years and still not reach anywhere near the farthest reaches of the universe.

Home.

It has been a long journey, and it's time to go home. Home to the most glorious and fascinating world in all of our explorations—Earth.

The Future of Space

Where did it all come from? Does it begin anywhere? Does it end? What's on the other side? Why does space exist anyway? So far we have been utterly incapable of understanding the grander meaning of space.

After centuries of study, we know so little. But the celestial frontier beckons the hearts of explorers more powerfully than any buried treasure ever did. Scores of dedicated scientists and astronomers are determined to find ways to cast light on what now lies hidden in darkness.

Perhaps you'll be one of those explorers who finds some of the answers we're looking for—the answers that will at long last explain what it's all about.

Theodore Parker, a philosopher, once called space "a handful of dust which God enchants." Wouldn't it be cool if one day scientists proved him right?

Glossary

apogee : the point of the Moon's orbit when the Moon is farthest from Earth.

asteroid : a very large rock in space, sometimes classified as a minor planet.

asteroid belt : a ring of asteroids orbiting the Sun.

astronomical unit (AU) : a unit of measurement equal to the average distance between Earth and the Sun, roughly 93 million miles (150 million km).

astronomy : the study of the universe, not to be confused with astrology.

aurora : the shimmering bands of light seen near the North and South poles of Earth. They are caused by solar wind particles entering Earth's magnetic field and discharging electricity. In the north, it is also called the aurora borealis or northern lights; in the south, the aurora australis or southern lights.

big bang : the massive explosion that gave birth to the universe about 15 billion years ago. The effects of the explosion can still be seen today by the motion of stars and galaxies, which are hurling away from each other at high speed.

binary star : two stars that revolve around each another.

black hole : a collapsed sun with such powerful gravity that not even light can escape it. A black hole is virtually invisible and can only be detected by the violent activity seen around it.

blue Moon	a rare occurrence in which a full Moon appears twice in one month.
bolide	see **fireball.**
brown dwarf	neither a star nor a planet, but a gaseous celestial body classified in between. Brown dwarfs are not associated with any solar system.
cepheid variable	a yellow supergiant that expands and shrinks every 3 to 50 days.
chromosphere	the very hot, reddish layer of the Sun, between the photosphere and the corona.
cluster	a group of stars sometimes numbering in the thousands.
comet	a large ball of ice and gas that usually orbits in a large disk of other comets around the outer edge of the solar system but may occasionally pass close to Earth and the Sun when its orbit is disturbed.
constellation	a group of stars resembling or named after an animal, object, or mythological figure.
corona	the outermost layer of the Sun's atmosphere.
coronal mass ejection	a massive release of gas from the Sun that discharges waves of charged particles toward Earth. It often disrupts satellite functioning and can even cause power outages.
cosmic year	the time it takes the Sun to orbit the center of the Milky Way, about 225 million years.
crater	a hole or depression on the surface of a planet or moon, caused by the impact of an asteroid or large meteorite.
eclipse	the obscuring of one celestial object, such as the Sun, by another, such as the Moon.
ecliptic	the invisible path the Sun and planets appear to follow across the sky.
fireball	a fiery meteor; also called a bolide.
galaxy	a very large conglomeration of stars, sometimes numbering in the billions or even trillions.
gas giant	a planet composed mostly of gas, such as Jupiter or Saturn.
geocentric	Earth-centered.
Great Red Spot	a massive perpetual storm seen on the surface of Jupiter.

greenhouse effect	rising temperatures from heat trapped by a thick, permanent cloud cover, such as found on Venus.
heliocentric	Sun-centered.
hydrogen	the most common element in the universe. The Sun's primary gas.
interferometer	two or more optical telescopes combined to bring a celestial object into sharper focus. Also, two or more radio telescopes combined to magnify radio (electromagnetic) waves from space.
Kuiper Belt	located along the outer edge of the solar system, a large region of comets and comet fragments that orbit the Sun.
light-year	a unit of astronomical measurement. One light-year is the distance a beam of light travels in one year, approximately 5.9 trillion miles (9.5 trillion km).
magnitude	the degree of brightness of a star or other celestial object as seen from Earth.
mare (plural *maria*)	a large black plain on the Moon, once mistaken for a sea.
meteor	a rock fragment from space and the streak of light it makes as it enters Earth's atmosphere and burns up; incorrectly called by some a shooting star.
meteorite	a rock fragment from space that survives the plummet through Earth's atmosphere and actually hits Earth.
meteoroid	any solid body smaller than an asteroid traveling through space.
Milky Way	the spiral galaxy we live in. Also, the section of the spiral arm of our galaxy that we can see in the night sky.
nebula	a gas cloud, often associated with newborn stars or stars that are dying out.
neutron star	the extremely dense and compacted core of a collapsed star. It may measure as small as 12 miles (19 km) in diameter and spin as rapidly as 30 times per second. When a neutron star gives off detectable radio signals, it is called a pulsar.
new Moon	a phase in which the side of the Moon facing Earth is completely in shadow.
northern lights	see **aurora.**
nuclear reaction	a splitting or a fusion of atoms, producing a massive release of energy.

Oort Cloud	a vast belt or disk of comets located in the outermost reaches of the solar system.
optical telescope	an instrument that uses mirrors or lenses to bring distant objects into sharper focus.
orbit	the elliptical path one object follows around another.
parsec	an astronomical unit of measurement equaling 3.26 light-years.
perigee	the point of the Moon's orbit when it is closest to Earth.
photosphere	the outermost visible layer of the Sun.
planetesimal	any of the large or small rocky bodies that came together to form the planets.
plasma	an electrically charged, gaslike substance emitted by the Sun.
pulsar	a neutron star that emits radio waves.
quasar	any one of the large and superbright quasi-stellar objects seen at the edge of the known universe.
radiant	the point in the sky from which a meteor shower appears to originate.
radio astronomy	the science of gathering and studying radio (electromagnetic) waves from space.
radio telescope	a large, dish-shaped telescope that gathers radio (electromagnetic) waves from space.
ray	on the Moon, a line of light-colored matter ejected by the impact of an asteroid and radiating out from a crater.
red giant	a dying sun that has exhausted its supply of hydrogen and begun to consume its remaining helium gases. It swells to gargantuan size in the process.
resolve	to bring into clear focus.
satellite	a natural or artificial object that maintains an orbit around a planet or other celestial body.
SETI	Search for Extraterrestrial Intelligence. A scientific organization that carries out radio searches for extraterrestrial life.
shooting star	see **meteor.**
sigmoid	an S-shaped formation of plasma on the Sun that scientists watch for to predict a coronal mass ejection.

Sol	our Sun
solar flare	a discharge of a massive stream of plasma, cosmic rays, X rays, and gamma rays from the Sun into space.
solar system	the Sun and all the planets, moons, asteroids, comets, and debris that orbit around it.
solar wind	a flow of charged plasma emitted from the Sun's outer atmosphere.
southern lights	see **aurora.**
spectroscope	an instrument astronomers use to separate light into its component colors, creating a spectrum that can be analyzed to determine what elements a celestial body is made of.
star	a giant ball of gas that generates energy from nuclear fusion reactions.
sunspot	a dark, cool splotch on the Sun. Temporary in nature, it is formed by magnetic disturbances in the Sun's photosphere.
supernova	an explosion of a star that dramatically increases in brightness.
variable star	a star that varies in brightness.
white dwarf	a star that has evolved beyond its red giant stage, has collapsed into itself, and has begun to cool.
zodiac	the 12 constellations aligned along the ecliptic, along which most of the planets travel.
zodiacal light	a cloud of space dust illuminated by sunlight that can sometimes be seen from Earth.

Index

acid rain, 39
alien signals, 101
Alpha Centauri (star), 75
Andromeda Galaxy, 66, 88–89
Angry Red Planet, The (video), 44
Antares (star), 73, 74, 93
apogee, 109
Arcturus (star), 75
artificial satellites, 22, 68, 112
asteroid belt, 45, 109
asteroids, 24, 44–47, 109
   impact craters, 9–10, 41, 110, 112
   name origins, 77
astronomical unit (AU), 66, 109
astronomy.com, 98
atmosphere
   Earth vs. Venus, 37, 38
   greenhouse effect, 35
   of habitable planet, 101
   of Jupiter, 48
   layers, 19
   of Mars, 42
aurora, 21, 109
aurora australis, 21, 109
aurora borealis, 21, 109

bacteria, 42, 44
Betelgeuse (star), 18, 72, 73, 91–92
big bang, 69, 109
Big Dipper, 76, 83, 88
binary stars, 72, 109
binoculars, 13, 15, 40, 79
black holes, 79, 81–82, 109
blue Moon, 14, 110
blue stars, 72
bolide. *See* fireball
Bradbury, Ray, 44
brown dwarfs, 82–83, 100, 110

Callisto (Jupiter moon), 51
canals, Mars, 42
Canopus (star), 75
canyons, Mars, 43
carbon dioxide, 38, 42, 43, 44, 62, 101
cepheid variable, 72, 110
charged particles, 24
Charon (Pluto moon), 60
chromosphere, 19, 110
cloud cover, 35, 37, 39, 111
cluster, 110
colored stars, 73

comets, 24, 60–64, 95
  defined, 45, 110
  name origins, 77
  Oort Cloud, 61, 112
constellations, 53, 64, 75–79,
    93–95, 110
  zodiac, 53, 113
Copernicus, Nicholas, 24
corona, 19, 26, 110, 112
coronagraph, 83
coronal mass ejections, 22, 110
cosmic rays, 20, 113
cosmic year, 25, 110
craters, 9, 10–11, 13, 37, 40–41,
    110
  dinosaur extinction, 46
  rays, 10, 112
crescent Moon, 7, 15

debris, 62, 64, 113
Deimos (Mars moon), 40
dinosaur extinction, 46
distance, 66
dust
  comet composition, 62
  Mars sky, 41
  meteor lanes, 64
  sunset brilliance, 27
  zodiacal light, 113

Earth
  asteroid collision, 45–47
  brown dwarf, 83
  craters, 10–11
  gravity, 6, 13
  greenhouse effect, 35–36
  Mars close appoach, 40
  meteorite impact, 45, 64, 66,
    111
  Moon and, 6–7, 109
  rotation/orbit speeds, 54
  "roundness" of, 14, 16
  Sun and, 24–26, 28
  tides, 13
  Venus differences, 37–38
earthshine, 15

eccentricity of orbit, 38
eclipse, 110
  lunar, 8–9
  solar, 26
ecliptic, 53
electric charge, 112
electricity, 109
electromagnetic waves, 111
elliptical galaxies, 87
elliptical orbits, 38
equator, 27
Eta Aquarids, 65
Europa (Jupiter moon), 51
extinctions, 46
extrasolar planets, 99–101
extraterrestrial life, 42, 44,
    100–106

fireball, 110
fossilized bacteria, 42, 44
full Moon, 7, 14, 110

galaxies, 1–2, 85–89, 110
  black hole, 82
  motion, 109
  types, 87
  See also Milky Way
Galileo Galilei, 24
Galileo spacecraft, 51
gamma rays, 20, 113
gas cloud. See nebula
gas giant, 48, 110
Geminids, 65
geocentric, 24, 110
G force. See gravity
gravity (G force)
  black holes, 79, 81, 109
  dead stars, 1
  effects of, 6, 30
  extrasolar planets, 100
  Moon, 6, 12–13, 15
  space travel challenges, 6
  Sun, 6, 27
  weight chart, 52
Great Red Spot, 50, 110
greenhouse effect, 35–36, 111

Hale-Bopp comet, 62
Halley's comet, 62, 63
heliocentric, 24, 111
helium, 23, 27, 28, 48, 50, 112
Hellas (Mars crater), 40–41
Herschel, William, 55
Horsehead Nebula, 92–93
Hubble Space Telescope, 68, 80,
    83
hydrogen, 17–18, 23, 27, 28,
    111
  Jupiter, 48, 50
  red giant, 112
  Saturn, 52

ice caps, Mars, 43
interferometers, 80, 111
International Space Station, 68
iridium, 46
iridium communications
    satellites, 68

Jansky, Karl, 81
Jupiter, 1, 48–52, 101
  as gas giant, 48, 110
  Great Red Spot, 50, 110
  ring, 50

Kappa cygnids, 65
Kuiper Belt, 60–61, 111

laser beams, 101
Leonids, 65
light
  aurora, 21, 109
  bending of, 28
  Moon, 13
  planet reflected, 1, 100
  speed of, 3, 6, 17
  sun and star, 18–19
  See also sunlight
light pollution, 97
light spectrum, 101
light-year, 58, 66, 111
liquid metallic hydrogen, 48
liquid molecular hydrogen, 48

lunar eclipse, 8–9, 110
Lyrids, 65

magnetic field, 21, 109
magnitude, 74, 111
mare (maria), 11, 111
Mars, 1, 40–44
Mars Orbital Camera, 43
Martian Chronicles, The
    (Bradbury), 44
mass-gravity relationship, 52
measurements, 66
    light-year, 58, 66, 111
    of neutron star, 111
Mercury, 31–32
Messier objects, 95
Meteor Crater (Ariz.), 10–11
meteorites, 64, 66, 111
    craters, 9–10, 66, 110–111
    from Mars, 42, 44
meteoroids, 45, 111
meteors, 45, 64–66, 110, 111
meteor shower, 64, 65, 112
methane, 55–56, 101
methanogens, 44
Milky Way, 85–87, 94, 111
    Sun orbit time, 25, 110
mobile, solar system, 66–67
Moon, 5, 5–16
    apogee, 109
    blue, 14, 110
    earthshine, 15
    eclipsed by Sun, 8–9, 110
    eclipse of Sun, 26
    far side, 12–13
    gravity, 6, 12–13, 15
    maria, 11, 111
    new, 6, 111
    orbit of, 6, 15–16
    origin of, 14
    peregee, 112
    phases, 6–9, 15, 110
    rising of, 16
moons, 24, 113
    Jupiter, 50, 51
    Mars, 40

Pluto, 60
Saturn, 53, 54
Uranus, 56
moonscape, 9–12
moth swarms, 103

name origins, 77
NASA Near Earth Object, 46, 47
nebula, 90, 95, 111
Nemesis Hypothesis, 83
Neptune, 48, 56–57
neutron stars, 72, 111
new Moon, 6, 7, 111
    as blue Moon, 14, 110
    solar eclipse, 26
northern lights, 21, 109
North Star, 77
nuclear reactions, 18, 111
    Sun and, 23, 27

oceans, 39, 51
omens, comets as, 62
Oort Cloud, 61, 83, 112
optical telescopes, 80, 112
    interferometer, 111
orbit, 6, 112
Orion, 78, 90–93, 95, 96
Orionids, 65
Orion's Belt, 90–92
outer space, 69–83
oxygen, 38, 101

parsec, 66, 112
Pathfinder probe, 42
"Peekskill Fireball," 64
perigee, 112
Perseids, 65
Phobos (Mars moon), 40
photosphere, 19, 112
    sunspot, 113
photosynthesis, 22
planetesimal, 45, 112
planets, 1, 23, 31–44, 48–60
    asteroid collisions, 45
    ecliptic, 53
    extrasolar, 99–101

formation, 28–29
gas giants, 48, 110
gravity generation, 6
life potential, 100–105
orbits, 38
stars vs., 1, 53
weight/gravity chart, 52
plant life, 38
plasma, 24, 112
Pleiades, 78–79, 83
Pluto, 51, 58–60
    orbit, 38, 57
Pope, Alexander, 56
Proxima Centauri, 72, 83
pulsars, 72, 111, 112

quasars, 89, 112

radiant, 64, 112
radiation, 20–21, 72, 113
radio astronomy, 81, 112
radio signals, 101, 111
radio telescopes, 80, 81, 111,
    112
radio waves, 111
rays, 10, 112
Reber, Grote, 81
red giants, 72, 73, 112
resolve, 35, 112
retrograde motion, 39
rings
    Jupiter, 50
    Saturn, 52–53
rocket, building own, 33–35
rock "face" (Mars), 43

Sagittarius, 93–95
satellites, 22, 68, 112
Saturn, 1, 52–54
    as gas giant, 48, 110
science fiction, 44
Scorpius, 73–74
seasons, 25
SETI (Search for Extraterrestrial
    Intelligence), 101–105, 112
Shakespeare, William, 56

shooting star. *See* meteors
sight catalog, 96
sigmoids, 22, 112
Sirius (star), 75
smoke, 14
Sol (Sun), 19, 113
solar dust. *See* dust
solar eclipse, 7, 26
solar flares, 20–21, 22, 113
solar system, 3–83, 86, 111
  components of, 23–24
solar wind, 24, 113
solar wind particles, 109
sounds, 50
southern lights, 21, 109
Space Camp, U.S., 68
space.com, 98
Space IQ quiz, 96
spaceships, 6, 24, 37
Space Shuttle, 68
spectroscopes, 80, 100, 113
spiral galaxies, 87, 111
stars, 1, 71–83, 113
  binary, 72, 109
  black hole, 79
  brightest, 75, 79
  brightness, 111
  classification, 72
  cluster, 110
  collapsed, 111
  constellation, 53, 110
  dying, 28, 72
  ecliptic, 53
  formation of, 29–30
  magnitude, 74, 111
  motion, 109
  name origins, 77

planets vs., 1, 53
Sun as, 18
variable, 92, 113
white dwarf, 28, 113
See also constellations;
  galaxies
storms, 39, 40, 50
Sun, 17–30
  asteroid belt, 45, 109
  closeness to Earth, 25–26
  corona, 19, 110
  coronal mass ejection, 22,
    110
  cosmic year, 25, 110
  diameter, 18
  distance from Pluto, 59–60
  Earth relationship, 24, 25–26
  eclipse of, 7, 26
  eclipse of Moon by, 8–9, 110
  eventual death of, 28
  gravity, 6, 27
  Mercury's closeness, 31–32
  Milky Way orbit time, 25,
    110
  Moon and, 15–16
  origin of, 23–25
  rotation, 20, 27
  as Sol, 9, 113
sunbeam travel, 27
sunlight, 22–23, 27
  greenhouse effect, 35
suns, 1, 21, 110
sunset color, 27
sunspots, 20–21, 113
supernova, 72, 113

Taurus (constellation), 95

Teapot (star group), 94–95
telescopes, 80, 81, 111, 112
tides, Moon and, 13, 15
Titan (Saturn moon), 54

UFOs, 102–105
universe
  big bang, 69, 109
  geocentric, 24, 110
  heliocentric, 24, 111
Uranus, 48, 55–56
Ursa Major, 76

variable star, 72, 92, 113
Vega (star), 75
Venus, 1, 35–39
  UFOs confused with, 103
Viking 1 and *Viking 2*, 42, 43
vision, 48–49
VLA (Very Large Array), 80
volcanoes, 11, 14, 37, 41
Voyager 1, 50, 106
Voyager 2, 55, 106

War of the Worlds, The (Wells),
  44
water, 41, 101
weight/gravity chart, 52
Wells, H. G., 44
white dwarfs, 28, 72, 113
winds, Neptune, 57

X rays, 20, 113

yellow stars, 72

zodiac, 53, 113
zodiacal light, 67, 113